AIMR Conference Proceedings
Investment Counseling for Private Clients IV

Proceedings of the AIMR seminar "Integrated Private Wealth Management"

March 11–12, 2002
Phoenix

Ernest M. Ankrim
Fredda Herz Brown
Jean L.P. Brunel, CFA
Natalie B. Choate
John Philip Coghlan
Brian Diessner
Barbara R. Hauser

Janet T. Miller, CFA, *moderator*
Suzan Peterfriend
Lori R. Runquist
Louisa W. Sellers
Meir Statman
David M. Stein

Association for Investment Management and Research®

Dedicated to the Highest Standards of Ethics, Education, and
Professional Practice in Investment Management and Research.

To obtain an *AIMR Product Catalog,* contact
AIMR, 560 Ray C. Hunt Drive, Charlottesville, Virginia 22903, U.S.A.
Phone 434-951-5499; Fax 434-951-5262; E-mail info@aimr.org
or
visit AIMR's Web site at www.aimr.org
to view the AIMR publications list.

CFA®, Chartered Financial Analyst™, AIMR-PPS®, GIPS®, and Financial Analysts Journal® are just a few of the trademarks owned by the Association for Investment Management and Research®. To view a list of the Association for Investment Management and Research's trademarks and the Guide for Use of AIMR's Marks, please visit our Web site at www.aimr.org.

©2002, Association for Investment Management and Research

All rights reserved. No part of this publication may be reproduced, stored in a retrieval system, or transmitted, in any form or by any means, electronic, mechanical, photocopying, recording, or otherwise, without prior written permission of the copyright holder.

AIMR CONFERENCE PROCEEDINGS
(USPS 013-739 ISSN 1535-0207)

Is published five times a year in March, April, August, August, and September, by the Association for Investment Management and Research at 560 Ray C. Hunt Drive, Charlottesville, VA. **Periodical postage paid at Charlottesville, Virginia, and additional mailing offices.**

This publication is designed to provide accurate and authoritative information with regard to the subject matter covered. It is sold with the understanding that the publisher is not engaged in rendering legal, accounting, or other professional services. If legal advice or other expert assistance is required, the services of a competent professional should be sought.

Copies are mailed as a benefit of membership to CFA® charterholders. Subscriptions also are available at $100.00 USA. For one year. Address all circulation communications to AIMR Conference Proceedings, 560 Ray C. Hunt Drive, Charlottesville, Virginia 22903, USA; Phone 434-951-5499; Fax 434-951-5262. For change of address. Send mailing label and new address six weeks in advance.

Postmaster: Please send address changes to AIMR Conference Proceedings, Association for Investment Management and Research, P.O. Box 3668, Charlottesville, Virginia 22903.

ISBN 0-935015-86-8
Printed in the United States of America
August 2002

Editorial Staff
Kathryn Dixon Jost, CFA
Editor

Maryann Dupes
Book Editor

Roger S. Mitchell
Series Editor

Sophia E. Battaglia
Assistant Editor

Jaynee M. Dudley
Production Manager

Rebecca L. Bowman
Assistant Editor

Kathryn L. Dagostino
Production Coordinator

Kelly T. Bruton
Lois A. Carrier
Composition

Contents

Foreword iv
    Katrina F. Sherrerd, CFA

Biographies v

Overview: Investment Counseling for Private Clients IV 1
    Kathryn Dixon Jost, CFA

Financial Physicians 5
    Meir Statman

Global Diversification Is [Still] Good for Your Clients 12
    Ernest M. Ankrim

Hedge Fund Investing for Private Clients 20
    Lori R. Runquist

Managing Performance: Monitoring and Transitioning Managers 32
    Louisa W. Sellers

Improving Tax Efficiency with Derivatives 40
    Jean L.P. Brunel, CFA

The Diversification of Employee Stock Options 51
    David M. Stein
    Andrew F. Siegel

Strategies for Retirement Benefits in Estate Planning 60
    Natalie B. Choate

Succession Planning for a First-Generation Family Business 72
    Fredda Herz Brown

Future Strategies for Private Wealth Management 80
    John Philip Coghlan

Selected Publications 89

Foreword

Force equals mass times acceleration; energy equals mass times the speed of light squared; and absent frictional forces, a body in motion remains in motion—all are laws of physics. Inherent in these laws is the notion that the universe is moving and changing. And as inhabitants of this universe, we must, therefore, be prepared for change. But being prepared for change and actually experiencing change can be two separate issues. Investors diversify their portfolios to mitigate the potential effects of change, but actually seeing change occur can be harsh (especially when the change results in a sizable drop in portfolio value).

Notably, the laws of physics (the inevitability of change) have not been kind to equity market investors over the past few years, and high-net-worth investors are no exception. Nearly every investor's wealth has been negatively affected by the changing equity climate. Add to that the shifting sands of income and estate tax laws, as well as the differences in cultural/regional attitudes toward intergenerational wealth transfer and business succession, and the challenges facing private wealth managers become clear. Managers must not only confront the problem of achieving respectable returns in very volatile markets, but they must also counsel clients on how best to weather this storm within the framework of the clients' very specific goals and objectives. In addition, managers must understand and be able to explain the intricacies of the multiple wealth management vehicles available for managing private client wealth.

This proceedings brings together authors who are able to offer valuable insights on the aforementioned topics. They address private wealth management techniques, tax-smart investing, wealth-transfer issues, and the changing clientele in the high-net-worth market. Their guidance, advice, and market observations help clarify many of the changes that are rapidly occurring.

We would like to give special thanks to Janet T. Miller, CFA, of Rowland & Company, for serving as moderator at the conference. We also extend our sincere gratitude to all the authors of this proceedings for taking the time to help in molding their oral presentations into written articles: Ernest M. Ankrim, Frank Russell Company; Fredda Herz Brown, The Metropolitan Group, LLC; Jean L.P. Brunel, CFA, Brunel Associates, LLC; Natalie B. Choate, Bingham Dana LLP; John Philip Coghlan, The Charles Schwab Corporation; Lori R. Runquist, Northern Trust Global Investments; Louisa W. Sellers, Ashbridge Investment Management, LLC; Andrew F. Siegel, University of Washington; Meir Statman, Santa Clara University; and David M. Stein, Parametric Portfolio Associates.

The laws of physics, as we know them, cannot be changed. Consequently, we cannot alter the fact that the world, and its systems, invariably change. High-net-worth investors, and their managers, are similarly caught in this net of change, but keep in mind that change is often positive. Although change recently took the equity markets lower, it also took them nearly straight up for many years. The law of gravity is colloquially stated as "what goes up must come down," but perhaps the law of the optimistic equity investor is "what goes down must also go up."

Katrina F. Sherrerd, CFA
Senior Vice President
Educational Products

Biographies

Ernest M. Ankrim is director of portfolio strategy for Russell Investment Group, where he serves as the lead portfolio strategist and directs communication efforts. Before joining Russell, Mr. Ankrim taught economics at Pacific Lutheran University. He is the author of more than 20 Russell Research Commentaries on topics as diverse as performance attribution, commodities, asset allocation, and investor behavior. Nearly half of these articles have been published in such journals as the *Journal of Investing*, *Journal of Portfolio Management*, and *Financial Analysts Journal*. Mr. Ankrim holds a B.S. in economics from Willamette University and an M.S. and a Ph.D. in economics from the University of Oregon.

Fredda Herz Brown is a founder, managing partner, and senior consultant with the Metropolitan Group LLC, whose consultants assist in resolving the challenges and dilemmas facing family and closely held enterprises. Ms. Brown is the author of *Reweaving the Family Tapestry* and numerous articles on family enterprises. She serves on the editorial board of the *Family Business Review* and *Family Business Client* and is a founding board member of the Family Firm Institute. Ms. Brown holds a Ph.D. in social personality psychology from Rutgers University.

Jean L.P. Brunel, CFA, is the founder and managing principal of Brunel Associates, LLC, a firm offering wealth management consulting services to ultra-affluent individuals. Previously, Mr. Brunel served as chief investment officer of private asset management at U.S. Bancorp and was in the investment management group of J.P. Morgan & Company. He is the editor of the *Journal of Wealth Management* and the author of *Integrated Wealth Management: The New Direction for Portfolio Managers*. Mr. Brunel is a graduate of École des Hautes Études Commerciales in France and holds an M.B.A. from the Kellogg Graduate School of Management at Northwestern University.

Natalie B. Choate is an attorney with the law firm of Bingham Dana LLP. Her practice focuses on estate planning for retirement benefits. Ms. Choate is founder and former chair of the Boston Bar Association Estate Planning Committee. She is the author of *Life and Death Planning for Retirement Benefits* and numerous articles in various estate-planning journals. Ms. Choate has taught professional-level courses in estate planning and has been quoted in the *Wall Street Journal*, *Newsweek*, *Forbes*, and other prominent publications. She is a graduate of Radcliffe College and Harvard Law School.

John Philip Coghlan is vice chairman of the Charles Schwab Corporation and enterprise president of Schwab Institutional. He oversees Schwab's asset management products and services as well as Schwab's services for corporations and their employees and for independent, fee-compensated investment managers. Mr. Coghlan holds a B.A. from Stanford University, an M.A. in economics and public policy from Princeton University, and an M.B.A. from Harvard University.

Janet T. Miller, CFA, is a partner at Rowland & Company. She serves on the AIMR Board of Governors and is a member of AIMR's Public Awareness Committee, the Council of Examiners, and the Private Client Task Force. Ms. Miller is a past member of the CFA Job Analysis Survey Committee and served on AIMR's Education Liaison Committee. She has held the positions of president, vice president, treasurer, and secretary for the Atlanta Society of Financial Analysts. Ms. Miller holds a B.A from the University of Toledo and an M.B.A. from Georgia State University.

Lori R. Runquist is a vice president and senior hedge fund specialist at Northern Trust Global Investments, where she is the technical expert on Northern Trust's hedge fund offerings and customized products and helps clients analyze their needs in order to recommend the appropriate hedge fund program. Previously, Ms. Runquist worked at Hedge Fund Research, where she structured customized portfolios of hedge funds for institutional investors, hedge fund investment products, and fund of funds for high-net-worth private clients. She holds a B.A. and an M.A. from the University of Chicago.

Louisa W. Sellers is a managing director and client financial advisor at Ashbridge Investment Management, LLC. Previously, she served as a vice president and senior portfolio manager in the personal trust and asset management group at Wilmington Trust and in the private client services group at Morgan Stanley. Ms. Sellers' areas of expertise include addressing the multigenerational issues that relate to serving wealthy families and educating family members about investments and fiduciary issues. She holds a bachelor's degree in economics from Trinity College.

Andrew F. Siegel holds the Grant I. Butterbaugh Professorship at the University of Washington Business School, where he holds appointments in the departments of finance, management science, and statistics. Previously, Prof. Siegel held teaching and/or research positions at Harvard University, the University of Wisconsin, the RAND Corporation, the Smithsonian Institution, and Princeton University. His research interests include optimal hedging in futures markets, the modeling of yield curves, the effect of futures trading on the stability of returns, gaps in the human genome project, and the efficient use of conditioning information in portfolios. Prof. Siegel holds a B.A. from Boston University and an M.S. and a Ph.D. from Stanford University.

Meir Statman is Glenn Klimek Professor of Finance at the Leavey School of Business, Santa Clara University. His research focuses on behavioral finance and developing an understanding of how investors and managers make financial decisions and how these decisions are reflected in financial markets. Prof. Statman's research has been widely published and has been supported by the National Science Foundation, the Research Foundation of AIMR, and the Dean Witter Foundation. Prof. Statman is a member of the editorial board of the *Financial Analysts Journal* and has twice received the Graham and Dodd Award of Excellence. He holds a Ph.D. from Columbia University and a B.A. and an M.B.A. from the Hebrew University of Jerusalem.

David M. Stein is managing director and chief investment officer at Parametric Portfolio Associates, where he leads Parametric's investment, research, and technology activities. Prior to joining Parametric, Mr. Stein held senior research, development, and portfolio management positions at GTE Investment Management Corporation, The Vanguard Group, and IBM Retirement Funds. Previously, as a research scientist at IBM Research Laboratories, he designed computer hardware and software systems. Mr. Stein serves on the After-Tax Subcommittee of the AIMR-PPS® Standards Committee and the advisory board of the *Journal of Wealth Management*. He holds a number of patents, an M.Sc. from the University of Witwatersrand, and a Ph.D. in applied mathematics from Harvard University.

Overview: Investment Counseling for Private Clients IV

Kathryn Dixon Jost, CFA
Vice President, Educational Products

The degree to which private wealth management has increased in sophistication over the past 20 years is astounding, particularly in terms of the expanded investment knowledge of private clients, a greater awareness on the part of investment advisors about the issues that affect good investment decision making for private clients, and the availability of both quantitative and qualitative tools that allow for more tax-efficient decision making. The image of the private client has evolved from being almost exclusively a person of inherited wealth to being just as often a person of new wealth. This expanded definition has shifted the needs and goals of the typical private client—from a desire to simply preserve wealth to an equal emphasis on the importance of growing wealth; from simply generating enough cash flow to meet spending needs to a desire to monetize low-basis concentrated equity positions; from traditional balanced portfolios with laddered bond maturities to broadly diversified portfolios with allocations to hedge funds, real estate, and venture capital investments; and from hiring specialized professionals offering departmentalized services to forming family offices that either encompass a wide array of professional services under one roof or operate within a well-established framework of interconnected legal, financial, accounting, and tax-planning specialists.

As the number of potential clients for private wealth management services grows, so too does the competition for providing those services. Greater competition has lowered investment management fees, increased the number and type of firms vying for private client assignments, and made available to the individual investor previously institutional-oriented products and strategies.

Probably the biggest development in the field of private wealth management during the past 20 years is the much higher level of sophistication with which the ever-present pinch of taxes is addressed in taxable portfolio management strategies. Twenty years ago, only a rudimentary guess was possible as to the actual after-tax return of a particular portfolio switch. The idiosyncratic nature of each tax bite was not encouraging to those who sought to design analytical tools to sort out the true tax impact of a particular trade—what might be a long-term capital gain for Mr. Smith might be a short-term capital loss for Ms. Jones. How best should these individualized situations be handled? Not only does each portfolio decision bring with it daunting tax analysis, but that analysis is always subject to change as a result of trades not yet made and the fluid nature of the client's shifting tax liabilities. Moreover, the inconsistencies of the tax impact on a client's wealth make after-tax performance comparisons between managers, as well as versus a benchmark, a tremendous challenge.

Today, much progress has been made in understanding the investment goals and objectives of the private client. A greater recognition on the part of private wealth managers of the intertwined family and business issues of the wealthy investor is helping to make inroads in the establishment of long-term professional relationships with private clients and is aiding the manager in adapting to the varied needs of clients. This proceedings brings together some of the people at the forefront of developments in the field of private wealth management. Each author has contributed his or her own expertise on a wide array of topics, including behavioral factors that affect client decision making, investment management strategies, tax-smart investing, advising families and individuals on wealth-transfer issues, and the challenges associated with addressing the ever-expanding needs of a new clientele.

The Financial Physician

The term "private client" has become synonymous with high-net-worth client, and significant wealth comes with its own set of challenges for the investment manager, one of which is the unrelenting human drive for more status and more wealth. Consequently, Meir Statman proposes that while seeking to both preserve and increase their clients' wealth, financial advisors should enlarge their role beyond wealth promotion to include general wisdom related to their clients' well-being. Advisors can temper the stress that often accompanies substantial wealth, for example, by helping clients establish reasonable benchmarks and recognize the most common cognitive errors, such as overconfidence and hindsight bias.

Furthermore, advisors must strive to understand that clients' aspirations and fears drive their decision-making process more than any rational assessment of risk and return in their portfolios. In investors' quest for upside potential and downside protection, Statman cautions that investors usually do not think rationally along the lines of mean–variance theory. Only by recognizing this tendency will advisors be able to adapt to the role of being, in Statman's words, a "financial physician"—an advisor who can point out the significance of the trade-off between wealth and well-being and whose job is not limited merely to beating the market.

Management Strategies for Private Client Portfolios

In addition to honing their investor psychology skills, advisors might also heed the lesson of strategic diversification when it comes to the question of whether to invest in international equities. According to Ernest Ankrim, the latest finding that the correlation between non-U.S. stocks and U.S. stocks has risen does not necessarily mean that investors should avoid non-U.S. stocks. Likewise, the recommendation to invest in bonds instead of non-U.S. equities because of correlation trends simply does not make sense.

On the contrary, Ankrim contends, investors with long-term objectives who are not trying to time the market should stick to their investment goals and recognize that, even though recent correlation values have been higher than average, little evidence exists to suggest that the returns of U.S. and non-U.S. equities have become more similar. He adds that bonds should be added to an investor's portfolio to reduce overall portfolio volatility, not simply to replace non-U.S. stocks. Advisors who suggest otherwise are merely making a tactical call about a particular view of the future based on the outperformance of U.S. stocks versus non-U.S. stocks. As Ankrim illustrates, correlation patterns vary quite a lot over long time horizons, and even at high correlations, a serious chance for substantial differences in returns exists between these two asset classes.

Another investment vehicle continues to capture the attention of private clients seeking the lure of high returns—hedge funds. Lori Runquist highlights the changes that have taken place in this increasingly popular—and accessible—area of investing, namely, the risk-reduction potential that hedge funds offer. She points out that in the world of publicly traded securities, hedge funds are still the only way to boost portfolio returns in a down market. Nonetheless, despite the panoply of strategies available to hedge fund managers designed to reduce risk and maximize returns, many hazards await the unwary investor.

Runquist outlines the pros and cons of various investment structures and warns that even though most high-net-worth clients still choose fund managers via word of mouth, advisor and manager selection should take a more deliberate and studied approach. Investors should be particularly wary of manager platforms, for example, that tout a fraud-proof structure. And given the dearth of data on hedge funds, benchmark and strategy selection are fraught with potential risks, particularly those associated with leverage and manipulated valuations. Recent trends, such as higher fees, greater liquidity restrictions, and the unreliability of audits, pose additional challenges. Thus, cautious investors who take the time to scrutinize the risk–reward trade-offs are more likely to find hedge funds to be worthwhile investments.

Clients seeking to enhance returns might also consider hiring a consultant. Louisa Sellers provides a thorough discussion of her firm's role as a consultant in managing the performance of investment managers. As every investment professional knows, growing capital in good times, and preserving it through bad times, requires knowledge, experience, and depth. No single firm can be an expert in all areas of investing, which is why even the experts consult experts.

Sellers delineates the evaluation process her firm uses for selecting new managers and monitoring existing ones. Performing initial and ongoing due diligence on all managers is important, and both hedge fund managers and managers acquiring taxable portfolios require a particularly thorough analysis. Performance is vital, of course, but it is not the whole story. Certain catalysts for changing a manager can sometimes lead to the termination of a manager, but a manager's emphasis on strategy (style consistency) and on personnel (managerial continuity) are the most important factors weighed throughout the process. Given her firm's interest in the longevity of its managerial relationships, Sellers explains how her firm's thorough vetting process pays off in terms of the performance that is ultimately delivered to clients.

Tax-Smart Investing

Tax concerns are paramount in the private client world of investing. The U.S. tax code, for example, impinges on investors' after-tax wealth by requiring them to pay taxes when trading physical securities before realizing the alpha associated with the transaction. Thus, sometimes investors are hit with both a bad investment decision and a tax bill on that bad decision. Jean Brunel calls this dilemma "the curse of the taxable investor" and demonstrates how advisors can use derivatives to circumvent it by altering the tax treatment of selected components of return and deferring the tax consequences of the investment decision until after the alpha has been generated (or the decision proves to be unsuccessful and the loss is realized).

Along with the benefit of being able to alter the timing of the execution, advisors can use derivatives to segregate the decisions they make along three dimensions (strategic asset allocation, periodic portfolio rebalancing, and security selection) and to vary the execution of these decisions according to the investment instrument being used. Derivatives strategies are also beneficial because they allow the advisor to combat portfolio drift and offset the tax bite arising from the periodic rebalancing of the portfolio. Thus, even when important tax-law caveats and potential risks are taken into account, certain derivatives strategies can significantly improve after-tax portfolio returns.

Achieving diversification in a way that enhances after-tax portfolio returns is another problem that vexes private clients. To tackle the complex issues associated with clients whose wealth is concentrated in employee stock options, David Stein and Andrew Siegel provide a disciplined framework for assessing how the options affect portfolio risk and how taxes affect the option values. A client's decision about how much of his or her option holdings to exercise and sell must incorporate the tax implication of that decision, the fraction of the client's wealth that the options constitute, the price of the stock, and the time to expiration, among other parameters. Rather than focusing on the usual risk–return trade-offs, for example, Stein and Siegel recommend that advisors take into account horizon wealth, not just annualized return. A technical analysis of the trade-offs between different end-of-period wealth distributions, particularly one that incorporates dynamic decision making, can then reveal the advantages of diversification as part of a disciplined strategy that avoids unwarranted risks and retains the possibility of significant upside gains.

Wealth-Transfer Issues

Although the issues of client psychology, strategic diversification, maximizing returns, and tax management are all vital to managing private client wealth, an investment advisor who has familiarity with the intricacies of tax law and estate planning can greatly help clients when the time comes to transfer the client's assets to heirs. To that end, Natalie Choate provides a comprehensive overview of how to handle retirement benefits in estate plans.

Thanks to recent changes in the tax law, people can now save more money and keep it in their tax-deferred plans longer. And because of the rising number of retirees, advisors can look forward to having an increasing number of clients who require expertise in transferring their retirement plans, whether defined-contribution plans or IRAs, to their heirs. Similarly, advisors may now have more clients who have inherited an IRA. In all cases, Choate spells out why emphasizing the advantages of using the life expectancy payout method and plan-to-plan transfers, ensuring that beneficiaries are properly named, and considering compliance obligations are essential aspects of estate planning. Knowledge of strategies that can be used to defer the payment of taxes or to avoid taxes altogether through charitable giving is also useful for clients who want to make the most of their retirement benefits.

Retirees and beneficiaries are not the only ones seeking advisors with proficiency in managing issues related to transferring wealth. According to Fredda Herz Brown, families who share assets in "enterprises" are also a growing contingent. Families no longer simply sell their businesses and retire; instead, they are choosing to operate a variety of business ventures and are looking to consultants to help them establish a framework for managing the new enterprise as a family unit.

Brown explores the family business consultant's role in facilitating the process of developing a governance structure that reflects the various constituency groups within a family. By establishing regular family and shareholder meetings and instituting an outside board of directors, for example, family members can work together toward creating a structure for the family enterprise that goes beyond basic organizational issues and the running of the business on a daily basis. Once such a structure is in place, families can then make a graceful transition to the next generation of ownership and avoid the most common pitfalls encountered in succession planning.

New Clientele

Even though according to John Philip Coghlan every segment of the affluent market is growing, particularly the segment with $500,000 to $1 million in investable assets, the private client business seems to have stagnated recently, largely because of the popping of the market bubble, the subsequent recession, and the attacks of September 11. In this uncertain market environment, Coghlan argues that investment firms must focus on the client—the individual investor—to tackle the challenges that stem from two particularly influential developments—the rise of the mass affluent and the engaged investor.

Although these changes have created a market opportunity for many firms, a solid combination of advice delivery, information management, and technology will be necessary to adequately serve this new clientele. Clients are increasingly technologically savvy and want to be involved in the investment decision-making process. As a result, a sort of "democratization" of financial advice has occurred, creating the need for investment advisors to adopt the role of the "trusted navigator" in providing advice that is objective and independent as well as personalized and affordable. To acquire and retain this new breed of client, Coghlan maintains that firms will need to work toward having a more open architecture environment, increased portability, greater tolerance of clients' relationships with other advisors, and more sophisticated technology offerings.

Financial Physicians

Meir Statman
Glenn Klimek Professor of Finance
Santa Clara University
Santa Clara, California

> Financial advisors should think of themselves—and present themselves—as financial physicians. Investors bring to financial advisors their stresses, fears, aspirations, and biases. Advisors can help investors balance wealth and well-being by using the tools of wise physicians: asking, listening, diagnosing, educating, and treating.

The findings and insights of behavioral finance can be useful to financial advisors. As an educator, I often speak with financial advisors. "Imagine that you are meeting with an investor," I say, "tell me what frustrates you most about the client's expectations." Advisors' answers are not surprising: Investors want the highest returns, with no risk, no taxes, and no fees, and the really rich investors want even more.

What can advisors offer? They can offer potentially greater wealth, improved well-being, and a good balance between the two. Several years ago, I attended a meeting between a financial advisor and a potential client, a well-educated man who had just received more than $30 million from the sale of his father's business. His brothers and sisters had each received the same amount. The advisor was trying to help the man build a well-diversified portfolio composed of domestic and international stocks and bonds—a balanced portfolio with low risk that would deliver good returns over the long run. But the man was distressed. Confident they could pick winning stocks, his brothers and sisters had chosen concentrated portfolios. They ridiculed his ideas about well-diversified portfolios and were sure to laugh at him when they came out ahead. As I listened, I realized I was happier than this much wealthier man. I had much less wealth but much greater well-being.

Wealth and well-being, what makes people happy, what investors want, and what advisors can offer—these are the themes of my presentation.

The Financial Physician

Many investors want more than a balance of risk and return or more than simply enough money for a secure retirement and college education for the children. Many investors want to be "number one," to win the race, and to outperform neighbors or siblings—all of which cause stress. The man I just described was miserable even while holding $30 million. Success in investing is about status; it is about security; it is about life.

Financial advisors must be financial physicians. To the knowledge of markets, securities, and portfolios—all the lessons learned from the science of finance—financial advisors must add the qualities of good physicians: listening, hand-holding, and reassuring. Physicians promote health and well-being, and financial advisors promote wealth and well-being.

Listening. What are investors' aspirations, emotions, and thoughts? What do investors really want? Like a good physician, an advisor must *really listen* to what investors need and want. Suppose a client took to heart a comment made by his brother-in-law at the last family gathering that implied his brother-in-law was wealthier, and the comment still bores into him, even two weeks after it was made. This client does not want to discuss his angst about that comment with anyone—whether an old friend or a new investment advisor. So, how can an advisor uncover this client's true feelings? The answer is through listening, empathizing, and diagnosing, just as a physician does. Investors trust good advisors as they trust good physicians. And trusting investors are honest investors. What do investors really fear? Is it risk? Is risk standard deviation? Much too often advisors jump into questionnaires about risk tolerance and miss the real fears and aspirations of investors. Consider international diversification. Risk is not what is driving investors away from international diversification; nor is an increase in correlations between domestic and foreign stock returns. Investors are being driven away from foreign stocks by the miserable performance of such stocks in the past decade and the fear that more miserable performance is in store.

Stress and Status. Good investment advisors listen to clients to uncover their sources of stress. A recent book contains interesting articles about well-being, including a particularly intriguing article by Robert Sapolsky that compares the physiology of animals under stress with that of humans under stress.[1] Consider two humans sitting at a chessboard and moving pawns from square to square. Their heart rates and hormone secretions respond as though they are gazelles being chased by lions. What is going on? Gazelles experience hormone secretions that increase their heart rates only when under stress—the fight-or-flight phenomenon, but we humans tend to be under stress all the time. We worry about mortgages, relationships, and the thinning ozone layer, all of which are mysteries to the gazelle. This constant stress can cause actual physical ailments, such as heart disease.

We experience stress most often in environments of little predictability, little control, and little social support. The man I described earlier who was given more than $30 million had only one reasonable option—to invest the money. He was thus facing the unpredictability of securities markets for many years to come. Securities markets are an environment in which we have little control and a place where we find little social support. Indeed, in the world of investing, friends and relatives are more likely to be competing against than supporting one another. (Interestingly, studies on behavior show that brothers-in-law are a source of particularly great competition and stress.)

What reduces stress? Status reduces stress. We always compare ourselves with others. Are we richer than our brother-in-law? We also compare our current positions with our own past positions and our aspirations for the future. Are we richer today than a year ago? Are we as rich as we aspire to be? We are happy when our status is high relative to that of other people and to our own past, or aspired, positions.

Wealth is absolute. Status is relative. Although most people cannot imagine what it would be like to be worth $100 million, most can easily imagine what it would be like to earn an extra $100,000 a year. This fantasy might become an aspiration, and that aspiration brings with it the stress of knowing that "I am not there yet."

Status seeking is good for us as a society because it spurs economic growth and innovation. But status seeking is also bad for us individually because it spurs stress as it separates winners from losers. Moreover, status is not fixed. Declines in relative wealth can be rapid, and status can drop even if wealth does not. An entrepreneur who brought her company public and netted $50 million is happy until she discovers that her rival netted $100 million. I remember an old story my mother told me about a man who complains to his rabbi that his house is much too small for him, his wife, and their many children. "Bring the goat inside the house," instructs the rabbi. The instruction makes no sense, but the rabbi is the rabbi. A week later, the man returns to the rabbi to complain that now the situation is intolerable. "Take the goat out of the house," instructs the rabbi. Suddenly, the house feels big.

Reasonable Benchmarks. The story of the man, the rabbi, and the goat is valuable to advisors because it addresses the concept of benchmarks. Advisors have to adjust the benchmarks, or aspirations, of their clients (and themselves). Whenever a client says, "Gee, I am not doing as well as Joe; Joe told me he invested in XYZ stock, and he has done so well," the advisor needs to change the benchmark of that client so that she can see how far she has come in her own investing. Remember that status and well-being can depend on one's position relative to other people as well as to one's own past and aspirations.

Benchmarks and aspirations need to be reasonable or stress will inevitably rise. My wife and I just finished renovating our home, a giant project. The other day, I realized that our new kitchen is bigger than the entire apartment we had as students. That apartment serves as a perfect benchmark. I say, "Relax some, Meir, you are doing okay."

Lessons of Behavioral Finance. Why do we humans behave the way we do? The answer is that the forces of evolution have designed us to behave this way. Our brains have evolved as our other organs have. The brain evolved to have modules that perform special tasks, just as the heart evolved to pump blood. For example, an important task of the brain is rapid recognition of facial expressions, knowing whether someone is happy, sad, angry, or threatening. This capability is hardwired because of its importance for human survival and reproduction. The same is true for status seeking. But not everything that is hardwired or "natural" is useful. Our brains do not develop as fast as our environment, and

---
[1] Robert M. Sapolsky, "The Physiology and Pathophysiology of Unhappiness," *Well-Being: The Foundations of Hedonic Behavior*, edited by Daniel Kahneman, Edward Diener, and Norbert Schwarz (New York: Russell Sage Foundation, 1999):453–469.

modules that helped us in past environments can hurt us in today's environment. Status seeking is crucial to survival in environments where food is scarce. High status in such environments brings sufficient food and other life necessities. But status seeking often backfires in environments where food and other necessities are plentiful. Now, people with $30 million are stressed because they aspire to $100 million, as if $100 million is as necessary for survival as a daily meal. Similarly, the learning tools embedded in the brain are imperfect, and we are subject to cognitive biases when such tools fail.

Hindsight bias nicely illustrates cognitive biases. Hindsight bias fools us into thinking that we have known the future all along when, in fact, we knew it only with hindsight. Consider Warren Buffett. "Oh yeah? What about Warren Buffett?" is a common response to anyone who suggests that beating the market is difficult. Buffett is indeed a genius. But did we know Buffett's genius with foresight, when it would have mattered, or did we know it only recently, with hindsight?

Warren Buffett's Berkshire Hathaway returns first appeared in the CRSP database in October 1976, so Jonathan Scheid and I used that date to begin a comparison of the returns of Berkshire Hathaway stock with the returns of other stocks.[2] If investors had put $1 into Berkshire Hathaway on October 31, 1976, they would have had $1,044 by December 31, 2000; if investors put that same $1 in the S&P 500 Index in October 1976, they would have had only $30 by December 2000. Indeed, Buffett did much better.

What would have happened to the price of Berkshire Hathaway's stock in 1976 if people had known then, with foresight, that Buffett was a genius? Undoubtedly, it would have zoomed higher in 1976, lowering returns for investors who bought Berkshire Hathaway stock later, in 1980 or 1985. In fact, what is amazing about Berkshire Hathaway stock is how gradually its price rose. This slow rise is an indication that people have come to know that Buffett is a genius only in hindsight, not in foresight.

What about foresight in other investments? Mylan Laboratories, a producer of generic drugs, performed better than Berkshire Hathaway in the 1976–2000 period; investors who had put $1 in Mylan Laboratories' stock would have earned $1,545 over that period. Did investors really know with foresight that Mylan Laboratories would do even better than Berkshire Hathaway? Home Depot also did better than Berkshire Hathaway, and in less time. Did investors really know it all along?

Hindsight misleads us about the past, and it makes us overconfident about the future. When we, as investors, look back and see how well we "predicted" the past, we are fooled into thinking that we can predict the future just as well. We become overconfident.

So, investors who were overconfident in their bullishness two years ago may be equally overconfident in their bearishness today. The mind-set of investors simply switches from "now we are going to have high returns forever" to "now we are going to have low returns forever." But hindsight is not foresight, and perfect knowledge of the past does not imply perfect knowledge of the future. Financial advisors must know the range of cognitive errors and use lessons, such as that illustrated by Berkshire Hathaway, to help investors overcome them.

■ *Rational versus normal.* Behavioral finance attempts to describe the investment decisions we humans make. We are neither irrational nor rational. We are normal—intelligent but fallible. We have brains, not computers, in our heads. We commit cognitive errors such as hindsight bias and overconfidence.

Consider normal behavior in the context of portfolio management and the mean–variance framework. Given the range of securities—from domestic stocks to derivatives to exchange traded funds—how do advisors think about the place of each security in a client's portfolio? The mean–variance framework assumes that investors are rational in the sense that they care only about the risk and expected return of their overall portfolios. So, investors should not look at stocks, bonds, and cash as individual components to help them achieve their personal and financial goals; rather, they should look at the overall relationships among the assets in their portfolios, and correlations between assets are paramount. But are we mean–variance investors?

Analyses of the brain, intelligence, and human behavior have taught those working in behavioral finance that investors are driven not so much by their attitudes toward return and risk but by their aspirations and fears. This predilection was noted long ago by Milton Friedman and Leonard Savage, who observed that people who buy insurance contracts often buy lottery tickets as well.[3] From a mean–variance perspective, lottery tickets are not only stupid; they violate all norms of rationality.[4] They have a negative expected return with high risk. But a

---

[2]Meir Statman and Jonathan Scheid, "Buffett in Foresight and Hindsight," *Financial Analysts Journal* (July/August 2002):11–18.

[3]Milton Friedman and Leonard J. Savage, "The Utility Analysis of Choices Involving Risk," *Journal of Political Economy* (August 1948):279–304.

[4]See also M. Statman, "Lottery Players/Stock Traders," *Financial Analysts Journal* (January/February 2002):14–21.

lottery ticket that costs a dollar gives us hope for an entire week. All week long, we can think about how to spend the $150 million jackpot we might win ("Oh boy, what I will do with that fortune!"). And by the way, the fun of playing the lottery is not always selfish. We often think of how we might spend our winnings on others. The desire to play the lottery might be irrational, but it is perfectly normal. Playing lotteries (within limits) contributes to our well-being.

■ *Mental accounting*. Humans—investors—care about upside potential, and lottery tickets provide it. Call options and aggressive growth mutual funds provide it as well. But while we are looking for upside potential, we are also looking for downside protection. When clients talk about risk, they are usually talking about the search for downside protection. And when they talk about returns, they are usually talking about the search for upside potential.

We tend to compartmentalize the assets we use for downside protection from the assets we use for upside potential. In the old days, many people kept their money for rent, furniture, groceries, and so on, in separate jars. Today, we have the same mental accounting approach to our various pools of assets. For example, T-bonds are viewed as assets suitable for downside protection (to avoid poverty), and high-flying assets—not long ago, Internet initial public offerings (IPOs) and hedge funds—are thought of, or mentally set aside, for upside potential. In behavioral portfolio theory, the old notion of the pyramid applies. People divide their money into layers; the bottom layer is designed for downside protection (e.g., U.S. T-bills), the middle is for steady wealth growth (e.g., U.S. T-bonds and Blue Chip stocks), and the uppermost layer (the next hot investment, whatever it is), is designed to provide upside potential.

Investment advisors tend to see themselves accordingly. For example, some advisors consider themselves conservative: "We are here to provide downside protection. We want to make sure that your retirement income is secure. If you want wild upside potential, take 5 percent of your wealth and go play with it yourself. You risk it; you lose it."

My mother understood the principles of mean–variance portfolios long before Harry Markowitz thought of them. When it came to food, she cared about two things: nutrition and cost. She had little patience for the presentation of the ingredients on the plate. She used to say, "It all mixes in the stomach." This description is a perfect representation of mean–variance theory. From the perspective of the stomach (portfolio), food (investments) is just bundles of nutrition (risk and expected returns). Who cares whether the bundle is called IBM, Amazon.com, or Philip Morris? But most people do care about how food looks, smells, and tastes, just as investors care about the identities of the securities in their portfolios. Most people do not want to be served a wonderful dessert that is ground up to look like it will in the stomach. And most investors do not want to have their securities ground up into a bland "index" portfolio.

Sometimes financial advisors become so enamored of means, variances, covariances, and the other paraphernalia of the mean–variance framework that they forget that portfolios must be palatable. But even my mother, who focused on cost and nutrition, paid some attention to the presentation of her meals. She knew the meals had to be appealing or else a child would not eat them. As investment advisors, we should follow her example. We have to focus on clients' fears and aspirations. We must give them downside protection and upside potential. We can use a mean–variance framework to assure that the portfolio makes sense as a whole, from the perspective of the stomach, but the portfolio must also appeal to the eyes, nose, and tongue. It must have distinct components—money for Johnny's education, retirement, and to keep alive the dream of riches.

■ *Regret*. Risk has so many definitions that without further clarification, the word is almost meaningless. One definition of risk is the possibility of not having enough for essential outlays. If that is risk, then people with $30 million face no risk. So, why are they afraid? The rich are not afraid of risk; they are afraid of loss of status, and they are afraid of regret.

Regret is what we feel when we realize that we could have sold all of our Nasdaq stocks at 5,000. Although risk is about looking forward, regret is about looking backward. Regret comes when we contemplate, with hindsight, what we could have done but did not.

Why do we feel regret? Evolutionary psychologists say it is a useful learning tool. When we observe our past actions and their outcomes, we learn what works and what does not. The painful kick of regret says, "You should not have done that. Don't do it again." The problem is that a learning tool that works so well in a highly predictable world does not work well in a world where randomness rules. For example, when we treat friends badly, we can anticipate the predictable consequences and know that we will regret our behavior. The anticipated regret usually serves as a deterrent. But regret often teaches us the wrong lesson in the stock market, where randomness and luck rule. We feel regret because we chose a stock that proceeded to crash when, in fact, we were simply unlucky.

Regret is associated with responsibility. Investors in the throes of regret often try to soothe the pain of regret by shifting responsibility to the nearest person. Often, this person is the advisor. "I didn't choose foreign stocks," say investors after foreign stocks post miserable returns, "My advisor chose them for me."

■ *Self-control.* The ability to learn self-control, like the ability to learn a language, is hardwired. But unlike language, self-control must be taught. Children may not be as eager to embrace self-control as they are to learn a language, but self-control has to be taught by parents because the ability to postpone pleasure is crucial for life. Advisors must extend the self-control lessons of parents.

Self-control is especially challenging for young or new investors, such as actors or athletes, who receive huge amounts of money at young ages. Investment advisors sometimes resort to drastic solutions, such as doling out an allowance to the client while keeping the bulk of the money under their control.

And lest one think self-control problems affect only young wealthy people, think about the rest of us. Social security, 401(k) plans, and IRAs—any pool of money that cannot be touched without penalty until some advanced age—are mechanisms to help us control the urge to spend.

But there is such a thing as too much self-control. Some clients need to be persuaded to spend more. Some people in their 70s and 80s insist on saving and feel financially insecure despite their $30 million portfolios. Advisors can help such clients relax the purse strings a little; a cruise around the world, for example, would not break the bank.

Wealth and Well-Being among the Very Wealthy. Some events in life bring a person both greater wealth and greater well-being. For example, Panel A of **Figure 1** shows the efficient frontier for an entrepreneur who just brought her company to market in an IPO. She has moved up the wealth axis and the well-being axis. She now has a greater amount of money and a greater sense of pride and achievement.

Once the wealthy (and the rest of us) are on the efficient frontier between wealth and well-being, however, they face trade-offs. They can have more well-being, but only if they deplete their wealth. Admiration enhances the well-being of the wealthy, but the wealthy we admire are the ones who contribute wealth to worthy causes. People admire Rockefeller and Carnegie for establishing the Rockefeller and Carnegie Foundations, not for making lots of money from oil or steel. As shown in Panel B of Figure 1, the wealthy can trade off wealth for well-being. When they donate their money to promote health in Africa or to support their alma mater, they lose wealth but gain well-being.

Not all wealthy people understand the trade-off between wealth and well-being, and not all accept that society does not owe them admiration, or even respect, just because they are wealthy. One potential outcome is the "angry affluents" phenomenon, where people conclude that "as rich as I am, I am not rich enough." Some angry affluents have been stung by insurance schemes or phony trusts set up to avoid taxes. The outcome of such schemes is rarely positive—either from a wealth or a well-being standpoint. Financial advisors can point out to angry affluents that they can reduce both their anger and their taxes by donating money to a cause they really want to support. They will lose some wealth but will gain well-being.

Some wealthy worry that they are not wealthy enough, but others worry that wealth takes a toll on themselves and their children. Parents who used to worry about not being able to pay for their children's college education instead worry about their children turning into spoiled brats. Again, financial advisors can help investors and their children see the benefits of balancing wealth with well-being and can create structures, such as family charitable foundations, that facilitate that balance.

Conclusion

Conversations with clients often resemble the Gary Larson cartoon in which the man says to his dog, "Ginger, I have had it! Stay out of the garbage, Ginger. Understand, Ginger? Stay out of the garbage, or else!" And Ginger hears: "Blah blah blah, Ginger. Blah blah blah, Ginger. Blah blah blah, Ginger." Financial advisors say, "High returns cannot be guaranteed. No one can guarantee that high risk will bring high returns. No guarantee, you understand?" And clients hear: "Blah blah blah high returns. Blah blah blah no risk. Blah blah blah guaranteed!" Conversations with clients can be frustrating.

Remember that investing is about more than money. It is about reducing stress in an environment—the securities markets—that creates large amounts of stress. Advisors need to remember the story of the man, the rabbi, and the goat to maintain their perspective.

Follow the pattern of the physician: Ask, listen, diagnose, educate, and treat. Financial advisors who act as financial physicians combine the science of finance and securities with the ability to empathize with and guide clients—thinking not about risk and return but about investors' fears, aspirations, and the errors they are likely to make. Financial advisors promote wealth and well-being just as physicians promote health and well-being.

Life does not resemble the Olympic games, and there are better goals than being first at the finish line. Remind clients, "Who cares if your brother or sister has $31 million and you have only $30 million? You have more than you could possibly need for anything you might reasonably desire. If your desire to outrun your siblings is so strong that it causes you to collapse midway through the marathon called life, what good is $31 million? The real goal is to get to the finish line in one piece."

Figure 1. Wealth and Well-Being Efficient Frontier

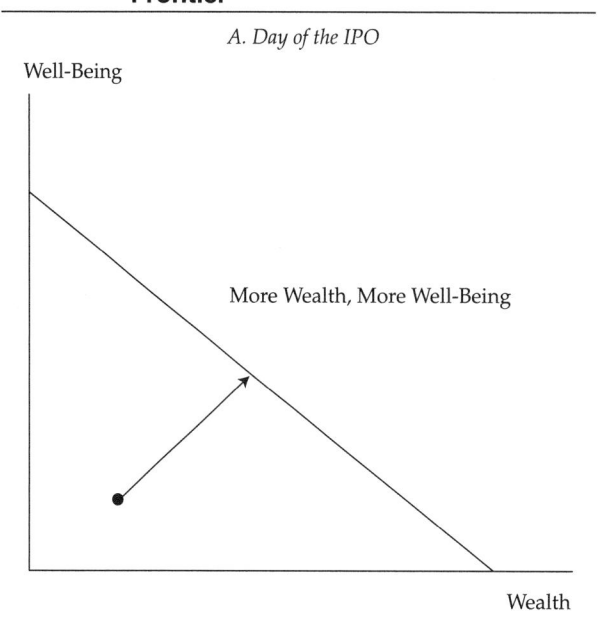

A. Day of the IPO

More Wealth, More Well-Being

B. Later, after Donating Money to a Charity

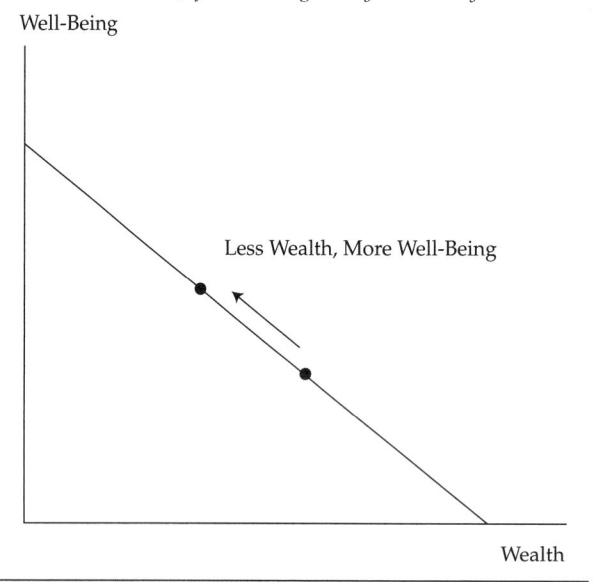

Less Wealth, More Well-Being

Question and Answer Session

Meir Statman

Question: How are young investors different from old ones?

Statman: When we are young, competition drives our consumption habits. We want sports cars and other toys. Advisors must help investors regain self-control and reduce consumption. Advisors know that young people cannot live without toys altogether, but they must set savings structures so they can afford necessities, including cars, when they are older.

Older people have the opposite problem. Some become so good at self-control that they turn into misers. In *The Millionaire Next Door*, for example, the interviewer asks an older person about donating to charity, and the person responds, "I am my favorite charity."[1] Advisors must remind investors gently that life does not go on forever and help them give up some control—whether giving control of the family business to the next generation, giving money to charity, or learning to spend money on themselves.

Some people are too hot and need to be cooled off; other people are too cold and need to be warmed up. Such are the challenges that advisors face every day.

Question: Do you have any advice on how to overcome individuals' desire not to pay advisors their fees?

---

[1]Thomas J. Stanley and William D. Danko, *The Millionaire Next Door: The Surprising Secrets of America's Wealthy* (Thorndike, ME: G.K. Hall, 1999).

Statman: I think financial advisors have conditioned their clients to believe that financial advice is free. As financial advisors, you have encouraged the impression that you earn your fees by beating the market and the rest is a side benefit. I think the result is horrible because it puts undue pressure on you to beat the market when your real work is your work as financial physicians.

I do see some improvements. First, the move from transaction-based fees to asset-based fees is a step in the right direction, and second, there is nothing like a bear market to show people that they need financial physicians. The next step is for investment advisors to re-engineer the perception in the market that advisors are primarily market beaters; advisors need to teach plainly that they are promoters of both wealth and well-being, not just promoters of wealth.

In the heyday of the bull market I spoke to a group of financial advisors who asked, "How can we compete with the free advice being given on the radio, television, and Internet?" My answer drew on the analogy with physicians: You can get a lot of medical advice from the media also, but when you have a pain in your back, you see your own physician. If your physician says, "That pain is nothing, you just pulled a muscle, and it will go away in a day or two," you don't feel resentful about paying the physician's fee. You have gained the well-being that comes from knowing that the pain is not an indication of cancer and that you are not going to die soon. That information is a great service that is worth the fee.

Question: Money managers subject themselves to additional stress by ranking and comparing themselves with other money managers. Do you have any advice for helping to promote well-being within ourselves so that our personal well-being might flow through to our clients?

Statman: Money managers live with stress; teachers live with stress. Living without stress altogether is not only unrealistic but also probably not useful. The real question is whether we can bring it under control so that we can manage it.

The way to bring it under control is to put things in perspective and readjust our benchmarks. There are many benchmarks. One is relative to other money managers, another is relative to your prior year's performance, and another is relative to your aspirations. Think: "I cannot be number one all the time, first quartile is not that bad; yes, I lagged the market, but I did better than my peers; well, I didn't do as well as my peers, but my wife loves me."

Controlling stress and encouraging well-being depend on identifying the kind of race you are running. If you see yourself as racing against the market, then you are in a tough race. But if you see yourself as a financial physician to clients, then your race is easier to win and a happier one to run.

Global Diversification Is [Still] Good for Your Clients

Ernest M. Ankrim
Director, Portfolio Strategy
Frank Russell Company
Tacoma, Washington

> Many people, including the author of an article that appeared in the *New York Times*, are arguing that international diversification is no longer a good strategy for investors because of the rising correlation between U.S. and non-U.S. markets. But is this argument truly based on a strategic call, or is it a tactical call? The evidence points to it being a tactical call in strategic "clothing."

On 4 February 2001, the *New York Times* published an article that stated the following:

> The correlation between American and foreign stock markets has risen sharply recently. This ... reduces the benefit of diversifying a portfolio into foreign stocks. ... The American bond market, however, is now far less correlated with American stocks, making it a better choice for diversification.[1]

This article explained that J.P. Morgan Chase & Company, Merrill Lynch & Company, and other major U.S. investment management firms were reducing the international equity allocation in their model portfolios because they had observed that correlation coefficients between the returns of U.S. and non-U.S. stocks were moving to levels higher than they had ever been. The article went on to say that if U.S. investors really wanted to diversify away risk in terms of lowering the volatility—the standard deviation of returns—of their portfolios, they needed to hold U.S. bonds in place of non-U.S. stocks. The plain language version of the article's conclusion is that if the correlation between U.S. and non-U.S. equities rises, owning non-U.S. stocks is unnecessary because investors can get the same return pattern simply by owning U.S. equities. For those who believe that statement, my goal in this presentation is to convince them otherwise.

What Is Diversification?

The driving force behind diversification is ignorance. Investors diversify because they do not know what the returns of various asset classes will be over a given investment horizon. If investors truly knew what would happen in the future, they would not need to diversify. Investors could simply invest in the assets that they knew would make the most money. Investors diversify, however, because they do not know for sure which investments will perform best. In "Portfolio Selection," Harry Markowitz said, "Clairvoyant analysts have no need for the techniques in this monograph."[2] This presentation assumes likewise.

Strategic versus Tactical Investing. Before I continue, I want to clearly distinguish between strategic diversification and tactical allocation. Strategic diversification's purpose is to formulate a long-term portfolio that best fits an investor's objectives (considering both risk and return). Given that the future direction of the market is uncertain, strategic diversification assumes ignorance. That is, a strategic allocation is made on the basis of long-term market relationships and avoids trying to time investments into and out of asset classes. Strategic allocations should change only if an investor's circumstances change. Recent market returns should not cause a change in an investor's strategic allocation.

---

[1] Jonathan Fuerbringer, "Hedging Your Bets? Look Homeward Investor," *New York Times* (February 4, 2001):C1, C16.

[2] Harry Markowitz, "Portfolio Selection," *Journal of Finance* (March 1952):77–91.

I think that helping clients select an investment allocation is as similar to and as unique as helping them select a pet. The advisor wants to recommend a pet that will be a good match for the client. Some pets jump all over the yard and tear up plants; some people think such behavior is cute, but others think it is an irritation. Some people have small apartments, in which case a Great Dane might be a bad choice. The point is that the advisor's job is to try to find a portfolio the client can live with—one that does not dominate the client's consciousness every waking moment. Selecting the appropriate mix for the client is what I call exercising strategic diversification.

Tactical allocation is when an advisor designs portfolios aimed at exploiting a particular view of the future. For example, a portfolio might hold U.S. rather than non-U.S. equities if the investor expects U.S. equities to outperform non-U.S. equities in the coming months. At Frank Russell Company, we conduct some research on tactical allocations, but for the most part, the potential for error associated with tactical recommendations is so high that we are reluctant to spend much of our time, or clients' capital, trying to exploit those rare insights.

Differences in Return. I like to describe diversification in terms of differences in returns. If I have two asset classes and the returns from both asset classes are identical, I cannot possibly get portfolio diversification from those asset classes. Advisors, therefore, recommend that clients hold a variety of asset classes because the future performance of various asset classes is unknown. Diversification is thus recommended not because advisors think their clients will earn the highest returns by diversifying but because holding a variety of asset classes allows clients to avoid the possibility of holding a portfolio with the worst possible returns.

If only two securities exist, an investor holds them both because she has a sneaky feeling she might be unlucky enough to hold the worst returning of the two if she holds only one. Say the investor's investment horizon is three years. After three years, the investor says to her advisor: "I know you told me these securities had the same expected return, but one has been beating the stuffing out of the other. Why did you have me buy both the good *and* the bad performer?" The advisor answers: "You bought both because I did not want you to buy only one and have the one you bought turn out to be the bad performer, and I did not know which one the bad performer was going to be."

The greater the differences between asset class returns, the greater the pain of holding only the bad performer. The variation in return differences of two assets is a function of the *volatility* of the returns of each of the assets and the *correlation* of the returns of the two assets. If the volatility of the returns of the assets increases, then the chances of having a period with widely different returns between assets also increases. Think of the situation this way. If you roll one die, the possible numbers are 1–6. If you roll two dice, the possible numbers are 2–12. The larger the numbers (i.e., 2–12 versus 1–6), the bigger the potential difference between each roll of the dice. So, the chance of having bigger differences in returns increases as the volatility of the returns rises.

Furthermore, if the correlation coefficient between two asset classes rises, the magnitude of the differences in returns is expected to shrink. If you and I both roll high numbers (i.e., our rolls are correlated), we will have smaller differences, on average, between our rolls than if our rolls are uncorrelated (e.g., you roll low numbers and I roll all types of numbers). The same is true if the returns to one asset class are unrelated to the returns of another asset class. If they are highly related, however, the differences in returns for short periods of time are likely to be small. This concept—increased correlation of returns—is reflected in the logic of the *New York Times* article. The author of the article was assuming that *all other factors are held constant* and that an increase in the correlation between two asset classes would correspond to a shrinking of the difference in returns between the two asset classes. But sadly, the world does not hold everything else constant. I will show how higher correlations between asset class returns do not necessarily translate into similar returns.

Bonds Lower Portfolio Volatility

The author of the *New York Times* article recommended that investors allocate more of their assets to U.S. bonds. The author was right, but for the wrong reason. The reason bonds should be added to an equity portfolio has less to do with the correlations between the asset classes and more to do with the relative volatility of the asset classes' returns. The variation in portfolio returns is strongly influenced by the volatility of the returns of the portfolio's assets. Therefore, bonds should be added to an equity portfolio because bond returns are much less volatile than stock returns.

Figure 1 shows the volatility of the U.S. large-cap equity market (S&P 500 Index), non-U.S. equity market (MSCI Europe/Australasia/Far East [EAFE] Index), and U.S. bond market (Lehman Brothers Aggregate Bond Index) for 36-month rolling periods from 1970 through 2000 (these data include the period used in the *New York Times* article—1978 through 2000). Notice that the volatility of EAFE was

Figure 1. Volatility of Various Indexes: 36-Month Rolling Periods, 1970–2000

slightly higher in the late 1980s and mid-1990s than that of the S&P 500, but for the most part, the two asset classes exhibit similar volatilities. The volatility for the bond market, however, has been very low since the mid-1980s and has always been lower than that of equities. So, if an investor wants lower volatility in his portfolio (i.e., increased diversification), he should add fixed income. This solution has little to do with correlations. Thus, even though the author of the *New York Times* article was correct in his recommendation, he put too much emphasis on correlation as the source of risk reduction.

Correlation Trends

To understand why the author of the *New York Times* article was right for the wrong reason, consider the correlation trend he observed. **Figure 2** shows the correlation trend for the past 10 years using rolling three-year data for the S&P 500 and EAFE. In the early part of this period, the correlation varied around 0.4; at the end of the period, it was about 0.8. **Figure 3** shows that the correlation trend of the S&P 500 and Lehman Aggregate for the same time period drops from roughly 0.6 to less than zero. Thus, the correlation trends in Figures 2 and 3 indicated to the author of the *Times* article that investors should buy U.S. bonds instead of non-U.S. equities to diversify away risk in their portfolios. I have two responses to this conclusion. The first I already mentioned: The lower volatility of bonds, not the lower correlation, lowers the volatility of the portfolio. The second pertains to my description of risk—the possibility of getting the worst returns across asset classes that have different returns.

The *Times* article implies that because the correlation coefficient is high, investors should be indifferent about holding U.S. versus non-U.S. stocks in their portfolios. I have recently visited London, Sydney,

Figure 2. Return Correlation of S&P 500 and EAFE, 1993–2001

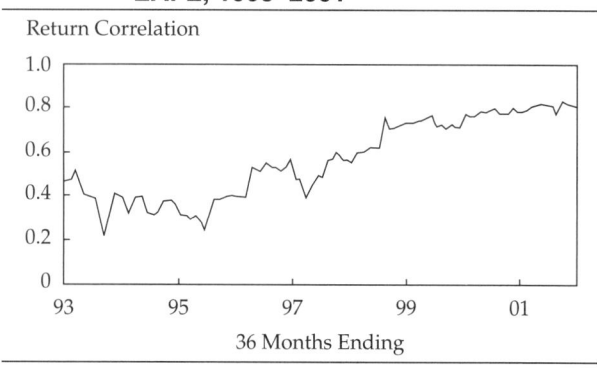

Figure 3. Return Correlation of S&P 500 and Lehman Aggregate, 1993–2001

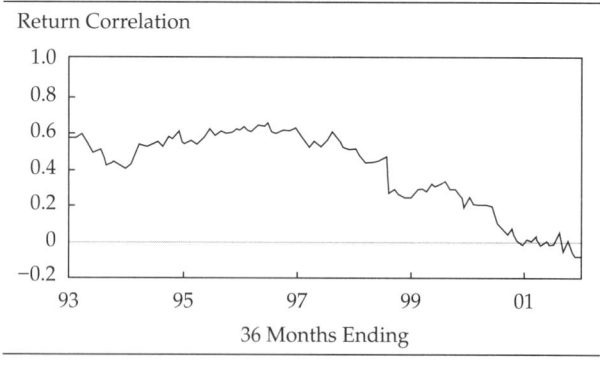

Tokyo, and Toronto, and the United States is the only country in the world where the suggestion is entertained that international diversification is unappealing because of rising correlations. Why? In the United Kingdom, Australia, Japan, and Canada, diversification means buying U.S. equities. The reality is that the U.S. equity market has recently beat the equity markets in all other countries, which is why investors want to buy U.S. equities. Nonetheless, U.S. investors might reasonably ask: "Is the *Times* article right on this diversification position and the rest of the world wrong, is the current correlation level unprecedented, or have the recent levels of return correlations changed the answer?"

The truth is that over a longer time period than the one used in the *Times* article, correlations are quite variable. **Figure 4** shows the correlation between the S&P 500 and EAFE for all the years that data are available for EAFE. Although the correlation is higher now than in previous years, the correlation has moved around over the three-year rolling periods: In the 1970s, the correlation ranged from slightly more than 0.7 to almost 0.1; in the 1980s, it varied between 0.6 and less than 0.2; and in 2001, it was above 0.8. Interestingly, when the correlation was as high as 0.6 in the late 1980s, no one recommended *not* diversifying outside the United States. Instead, advisors encouraged international diversification because everyone thought Japan would own the world. Why were people not paying attention to correlations then? I will show why shortly.

Bonds follow a similar pattern. The correlation between U.S. bonds and U.S. equities has jumped around, as shown in **Figure 5**. The correlation is low now but was also low in the late 1980s, when few advisors were telling investors to add more bonds to their portfolios to lower volatility. And why were they not making that recommendation? Aside from October 1987, the equity market was rising and bonds could not compete in terms of expected return. Investors did not want to hear that they should put more money in bonds.

Chasing Recent Performance?

If holding only one country in a portfolio was such a great idea, why would it not apply to other countries besides the United States? When I read the *Times* article, my initial concern was that the article would lead investors to chase the recent good returns of U.S. equities and to flee from the recent poor returns of non-U.S. equities. The reason given for the recommendation, however, was the correlation trend. In effect, market-chasing behavior was being encouraged in "correlation trend" clothing. To determine whether my instincts were correct in assuming that the author of the *Times* article was proposing return-chasing behavior, I looked at what was happening in the markets when the article was published. The highest correlation recorded in the *Times* article occurred for the 36 months ending July 2000. The 36-month correlation coefficient at that time was 0.78. The annualized return for the same three years was 16.4 percent for the Russell 1000 and 8.3 percent for EAFE.

Consider what would happen if the returns for this 36-month observation were reversed. What if EAFE had earned 16.4 percent and the Russell 1000, 8.3 percent? The correlation coefficient would be unchanged at 0.78. But if the returns were reversed, would the rise in correlation be viewed as a reason for abandoning non-U.S. equities? My guess is not a chance. Any investor holding non-U.S. equities would be glad to be holding them. Therefore, the correlation cannot be the reason behind the recommendation to move out of international equities.

I next looked at the annualized difference in returns for every 36-month period in the S&P 500 and EAFE. For instance, if the S&P 500's annualized return over three years was 20 percent and EAFE's was 16 percent, the difference would be 400 bps, or 4 percentage points (pps). Assuming that investors cannot predict which of the two series will have higher returns, I examined only the absolute value of that difference. My only concern was if the returns of the two series differed. So, 400 bps was the difference. If in another three-year period U.S. equities earned 12 percent annualized and non-U.S. equities earned 7 percent annualized, the difference would be 500 bps. I tracked this difference over time, as shown in **Figure 6**. Although market observers know recent correlation values have been higher than average,

Figure 4. Return Correlation of S&P 500 and EAFE, 1972–2001

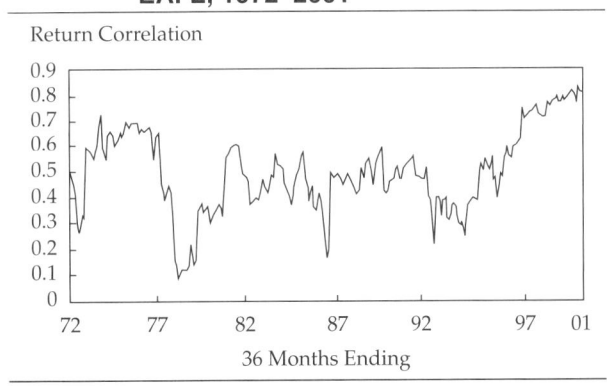

Figure 5. Return Correlation of S&P 500 and Lehman Aggregate, 1972–2001

Figure 6. S&P 500 vs. EAFE: Annualized Absolute Return Differences, 1972–2001

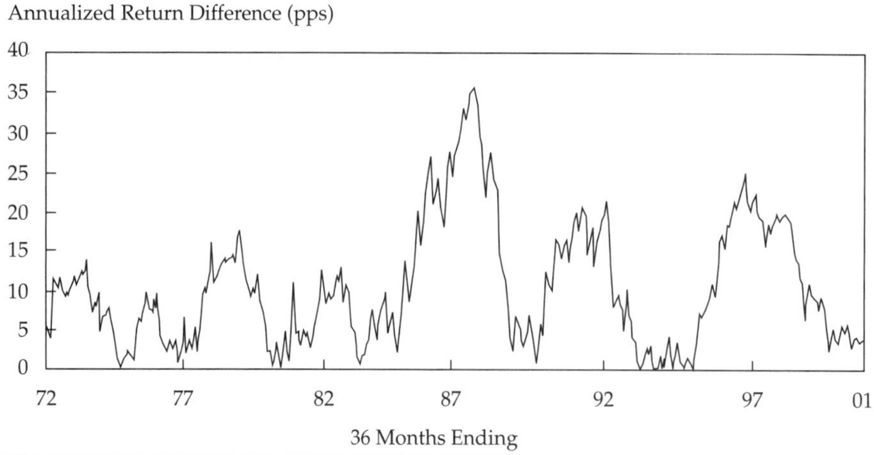

little evidence exists that the returns of U.S. and international equities have become more similar.

Next, I calculated the correlation coefficient between those two asset classes for every three-year period from 1970 through 2001. I sorted the entire data set into quintiles on the basis of the lowest correlation three-year experience to the highest and carried along the annualized return difference for that three-year window. I then took the average correlation of the observations with the lowest correlation between U.S. and non-U.S. equities and so on, as well as the corresponding average absolute return difference. The results are shown in **Table 1**.

Table 1. Correlation and Return Difference for S&P 500 versus EAFE: 36-Month Experience, 1970–2001

Correlation Measure	Average Correlation	Average Annualized Absolute Difference
Lowest	0.28	9.62 pps
Next	0.42	9.56
Middle	0.49	15.10
Next	0.58	9.85
Highest	0.73	8.55

The average correlation for the quintile of the lowest correlations is about 0.3, and the average correlation for the quintile of the highest correlations is about 0.7. The average difference between returns for the lowest quintile is 962 bps, and for the highest quintile, 855 bps. These results indicate that if an investor, not knowing which asset class would be the outperformer, happened to be in a three-year period that was in the top 20 percent of correlations between U.S. and non-U.S. equities, the annualized difference in returns would have averaged 855 bps, a big difference that is enough to grab any investor's attention. This finding means that a high correlation in returns does not necessarily imply similar returns.

I then wanted to see if any relationship existed between the correlations and the annualized return differences shown in Table 1. I found that the correlation between the 36-month correlations and the 36-month annualized absolute return differences was –0.08, essentially zero.

Next, I documented the correlation coefficient and the annualized absolute return difference for every three-year period. The results are shown in the scatter chart in **Figure 7**. One might expect the annualized differences to fall as the correlations rise. This expectation is the basis of the argument that investors should not buy non-U.S. equities when correlation coefficients are high because the returns are more alike. But that did not happen. And what if I assume no relationship exists between the volatilities in these markets and the correlation coefficients between them? What would I expect for a one-standard-deviation boundary? It would look like the dashed line in Figure 7. The one-standard-deviation line should have approximately two-thirds of the data points beneath it. But it does not. So, the distribution, at the very least, is not normal, and the assumption of independence is questionable too.

Now, here is a point I want to stress. Suppose the correlation coefficient between U.S. and non-U.S. equities is 0.3. Figure 7 shows that even if no relationship between the correlation and volatility of returns of the two asset classes exists, the annualized absolute return difference is expected to be greater than 1,100 bps one-third of the time (one standard deviation). And even with a correlation coefficient as high as 0.7, the investor still has about a one-in-three chance of the difference being 800 bps or more. The flatness of this one-standard-deviation line causes me to believe

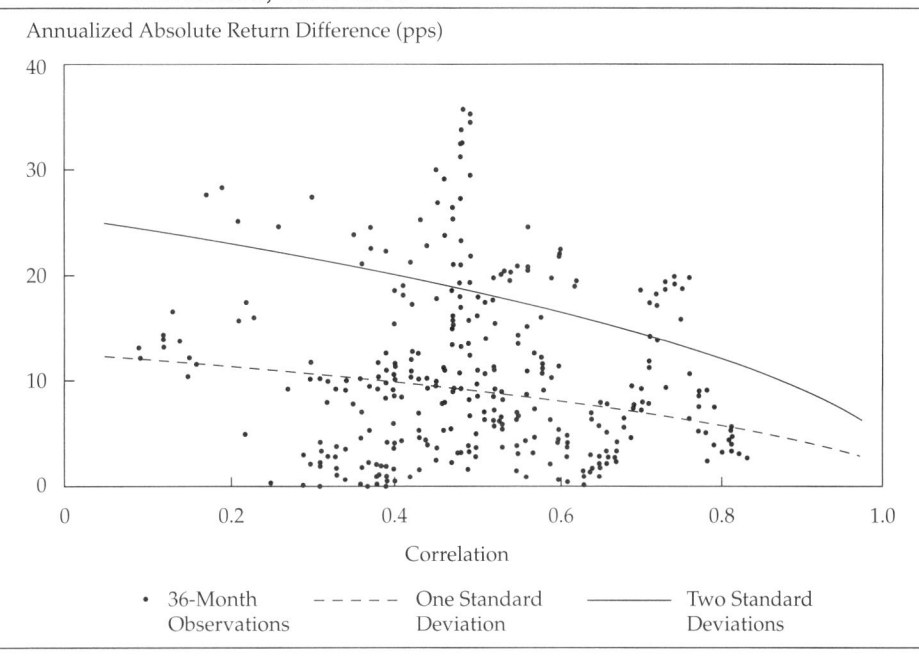

Figure 7. S&P 500 vs. EAFE: Annualized Absolute Return Differences and Correlation, 1972–2001

that even in theory, the importance of correlation has been oversold. When the correlation goes from 0.3 to 0.7, the one-standard-deviation line drops from about 1,100 bps to 800 bps, and 800 bps a year over a three-year period is surely enough to be of concern. I also graphed the two-standard-deviation line, which tells the same story: Even at high correlations, a serious chance of substantial differences in returns exists between these two asset classes.

Finally, I looked at the volatility of the markets to see how volatility related to the correlation experiences. I found that the correlation between the 36-month correlation in returns and the average of two 36-month annualized standard deviations was 0.41, which is fairly large. What does this finding mean? Remember, the variation in return differences of two assets is a function of the volatility of each asset and the correlation between the two assets. If only the correlation between the two assets increases, the return differences should shrink. But if the correlation increases during a period when the volatilities of the assets also increase, these forces (correlation and volatility) tend to be offsetting in terms of return behavior—a result that is consistent with my assertion that higher correlations are not necessarily associated with small or shrinking differences in returns. This outcome occurs because most periods of high correlations happen during periods of high volatility.

Conclusion

I could not find any pattern indicating that rising correlations should reduce investors' interest in holding both U.S. and non-U.S. equities. So, why is the question of international diversification such a hot topic for discussion at this time? I think I know.

Forget dispersion and think about which asset class has been outperforming recently. **Figure 8** shows the difference in returns between U.S. and non-U.S. equities annualized over the same rolling 36-month intervals used throughout this presentation. Any point above the zero line shows that U.S. equities are outperforming, and any point below that line shows that non-U.S. equities are outperforming. I mentioned that in the 1980s, correlation coefficients were just as high as they are now. Why was no one saying then that U.S. investors did not need to hold international equities? As Figure 8 shows, non-U.S. equities were winning the performance game in the mid-1980s, when advisors were pushing investors to expand the amount of investments they made outside the United States. Now the same degree of correlation exists between U.S. and non-U.S. equities, but this time, the general wisdom is to get out of non-U.S. equities. Figuring out why is not difficult.

I understand that the recent poor performance of international equities makes the idea of international diversification tough to sell to U.S. investors. But the pattern of longer-term correlations does not mandate an abandonment of this strategy. If investors are concerned about the classic definition of risk—the volatility of a portfolio—they can reduce risk by holding more bonds, not by changing the composition of their equity allocations. Furthermore, if they want to change the composition of their equity

Figure 8. S&P 500 vs. EAFE: 36-Month Annualized Difference, 1972–2001

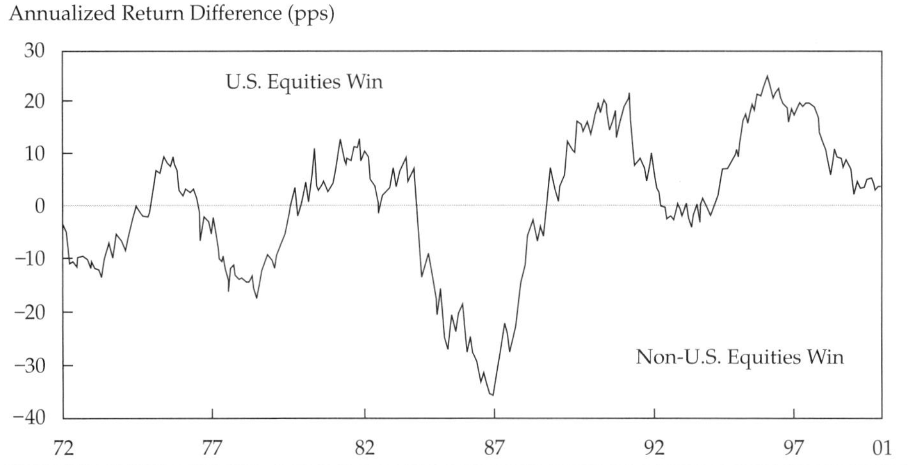

allocations, the recent patterns of correlation are of minor interest at best. The recent call to avoid international equities is based merely on a tactical decision that the U.S. market will outperform non-U.S. markets, not on a strategic policy recommendation.

My objective is to encourage a rational view of strategic asset allocation. I object to recommendations based on correlation patterns that appear to be strategic risk management moves when they are merely confirming the human tendency to run away from a painful experience that is really a tactical call. If the strategist is projecting that the U.S. market will outperform other markets, then the strategist should make that call. If the strategist is right, he or she will be recognized and rewarded. If the strategist is wrong, he or she will pay the price for that incorrect call.

Claiming that a tactical call to disinvest in international equities is a strategic move based on correlation patterns creates an unfair asymmetrical payoff. If the strategist is right, his or her clients will look back in three years and be glad they were not holding international equities. If the strategist is wrong, then as an advisor, the strategist gets to say, "Well, remember, this was not a return-optimizing strategy, we were trying to manage risk." If it is a tactical call, it is a tactical call, and if it is a risk-control call, make it a risk-control call. It cannot be a tactical call on the upside and a strategic call on the downside. If this recommendation not to hold international equities is a strategic, risk-reduction call, my observation is that this argument disguised in "correlation trend" clothing is incorrect. Advisors should call tactical calls what they are and manage risk in a disciplined, strategic way that can produce important, long-term results for clients, regardless of the latest correlation patterns.

Question and Answer Session

Ernest M. Ankrim

Question: Were your results distorted by Japan's experience, and if you had taken Japan out of EAFE, would that have significantly affected your correlation return data versus the S&P 500?

Ankrim: Yes, the results would be different if I had taken Japan out of EAFE for two reasons. First, historically, Japan has had a lower correlation with U.S. returns than the rest of the components of EAFE. Second, Japan's weight in EAFE has changed dramatically during the 30 years of data I used—from a high of close to 67 percent to less than 20 percent. So, excluding Japan would have a varying effect depending on the data period.

I would add, though, that cap-weighted indexes are rational. They represent investment opportunities that make sense. The idea that Japan represented more of the correlation in 1988 is appropriate because it constituted more of the market in 1988.

Question: Isn't geographical diversification irrelevant? Shouldn't investors be focusing on sector diversification in global markets?

Ankrim: Our data in terms of factor decomposition returns indicate that the country factor has declined in importance and the sector factor has increased in importance. Countries used to be the predominant explainer of returns, and sectors were relatively less important. Nevertheless, although countries have become less important and sectors have become more important, the absolute magnitude of each factor is now fairly close to the other. Even though sectors may be more important than they were 10 years ago, countries have not evaporated as a significant explanatory element of multicountry portfolio returns.

Hedge Fund Investing for Private Clients

Lori R. Runquist
Vice President, Senior Hedge Fund Specialist
Northern Trust Global Investments
Chicago

> Historically, hedge funds have attracted private investors with the lure of high returns. More recently, however, the risk-reduction potential of hedge funds has drawn the attention of both private and institutional investors. No matter the reason for investing in hedge funds, investors must carefully weigh the pros and cons of various investment structures and select appropriate benchmarks, strategies, and managers in order to be successful. Investors should also be aware of recent industry trends so that they can continue to take advantage of hedge funds' ability to outperform the public stock and bond markets and to provide a market hedge.

The nature of hedge fund investing has changed rather dramatically in the past seven years, particularly for private or high-net-worth clients. Although hedge funds offer tremendous opportunities, they also carry a great deal of risk; in fact, an apt subtitle for this presentation would be "Lessons in Hedge Fund Investing You Would Prefer Not to Learn First Hand." I will begin with a brief overview of why hedge funds are so popular and who invests in them. I will then share the lessons I have learned about some of the specific risks associated with hedge funds by addressing their investment structure and the issues to consider when selecting advisors, benchmarks, strategies, and managers. Finally, I will discuss recent industry trends.

Why Hedge Funds?

Private clients are interested in hedge funds right now for one main reason: Hedge fund investing is the only way to generate positive returns with publicly traded securities in down markets. Positive returns can be generated with real estate, commodities, and private equity in down markets, but with publicly traded stocks and bonds, the only way to generate positive returns in down markets is through hedge fund strategies.

Another important reason for the interest in hedge funds is that adding hedge fund strategies to a traditional asset allocation mix can enhance the returns and reduce the risk of the overall portfolio because hedge fund returns have a low correlation with traditional investments. In the traditional investment management world, the only thing managers can do when they anticipate volatile or declining markets is to ride out losses in their portfolios or go to cash, but times of volatility and market shock provide hedge fund managers with opportunities to generate positive returns. In particular, short selling provides downside protection.

Strategies. Hedge funds can use a variety of investment strategies: long–short equity, convertible arbitrage, fixed-income arbitrage, merger/risk arbitrage, event driven, distressed securities, emerging markets, sector specific, macro, and equity market-neutral investing.

■ *Short selling.* Long–short equity is probably the most familiar hedge fund strategy, but the characteristic that all hedge funds have in common is the ability to sell short.[1] In the long-only world, an investor buys an undervalued security expecting its value to rise. If it rises, the investor makes a profit. In the short-selling world, an investor can make the opposite bet, so if an investor thinks a dot-com stock is overvalued, the investor can short the stock. If the price declines, the investor makes a profit. This

---
[1] Short selling is the practice of borrowing a stock on collateral and immediately selling it on the market with the intention of buying it back later at a lower price. Short positions can be taken to hedge a long position or the market or as a stand-alone investment. Profits are realized with a decline in the price of a security.

ability to play the depreciation bet allows hedge fund managers to generate positive returns in down markets.

Short selling is used by hedge funds for two reasons. The first reason is simply to generate profits. The second reason is to create a market hedge,[2] which is the reason given by most managers who are aggressive shorters. For example, if a manager is long technology stocks, he may hedge his bet by shorting the Nasdaq. This combination of making appreciative bets while trying to hedge the downside drives the majority of hedge fund approaches.

■ *Arbitrage.* Many hedge fund strategies are arbitrage based. In the world of arbitrage, a relationship that normally exists between two securities temporarily becomes askew. The arbitrageur believes that the "abnormal" relationship will revert to its more "normal" state in the future and seeks to benefit from this imbalance by simultaneously purchasing and selling related securities to capture the profit that results by the correction of the temporary pricing discrepancy. Arbitraged securities can be fixed income or equity.

■ *Market neutral.* Market neutral is often viewed in broad terms as any strategy that generates a return independent of equity market movements, which includes all of the arbitrage strategies. Additionally, a common strategy is equity market-neutral investing—long positions matched by equal dollar amounts of short positions to hedge out the effect of market movements. The rationale is that if a manager is a dollar long for every dollar short, although upside potential is certainly limited, a cushion is created against a negative market movement.

Performance. Historically, hedge funds have outperformed the public stock and bond markets. From January 1990 to December 2001, the HFRI (Hedge Fund Research, Inc.) Fund Weighted Composite Index, which encompasses about 3,500 funds, outperformed the S&P 500 Index by approximately 3 percent and the Lehman Aggregate Bond Index by nearly 8 percent, as shown in **Table 1**. How are hedge funds generating this level of performance? In the past 12 years, hedge funds have outperformed the S&P 500 in 95 percent of the down markets and have exhibited lower volatility than the public equity markets have. **Table 2** shows that for the 24-month period when the S&P 500 had positive monthly returns greater than 5 percent, the average monthly return for the S&P 500 was 6.98 percent versus 2.80 percent for hedge funds. For the 22-month period when the S&P 500 had returns below –3 percent, the average monthly return for the S&P 500 was –5.74 percent versus –1.73 percent for hedge funds. These results illustrate the much lower volatility of hedge funds compared with the S&P 500.

[2]Creating a market hedge is the practice of taking a secondary position to offset the risk of the primary position—that is, to purchase a long position and a related secondary short position in a similar security.

Table 1. Relative Hedge Fund Performance, January 1990–December 2001

Index	Average Annualized Return
HFRI Fund Weighted Composite Index	15.9%
S&P 500 Index	12.85
Lehman Aggregate Bond Index	8.08
U.S. 90-day T-bills	5.14

Source: Hedge Fund Research, Inc.

Table 2. Outperformance of S&P 500 by Hedge Funds Measured by Average Monthly Returns, January 1990–December 2001

Monthly Performance of S&P 500	S&P 500	HFRI Fund Weighted Composite Index
More than 5% (24 months)	6.98%	2.80%
3% to 5% (22 months)	3.97	2.24
1% to 3% (34 months)	1.95	1.98
1% to –1 % (23 months)	0.08	1.10
–1% to –3% (19 months)	–2.07	0.60
Less than –3% (22 months)	–5.74	–1.73

Source: Hedge Fund Research, Inc.

Although in strong bull markets hedge funds will seldom, if ever, outperform the S&P 500 (by definition hedge fund managers always give up some part of their upside potential in order to hedge their downside risk), during market shocks and declining periods, hedge funds will almost always outperform the S&P 500. Because the downside volatility of hedge fund returns has been reduced so significantly as compared with that of the S&P 500, returns over the 12-year period have compounded to the point of outperforming the S&P 500 on an absolute basis. For example, **Figure 1** depicts a market shock. In September 2001, the Nasdaq was down 17 percent, the S&P 500 was down 8 percent, and hedge funds (HFRI Fund of Funds Index) were down about 1.5 percent. The ability to be defensive allowed hedge fund managers to provide investors with returns that were significantly better than those in the traditional capital markets.

Figure 1. Performance, September 2001

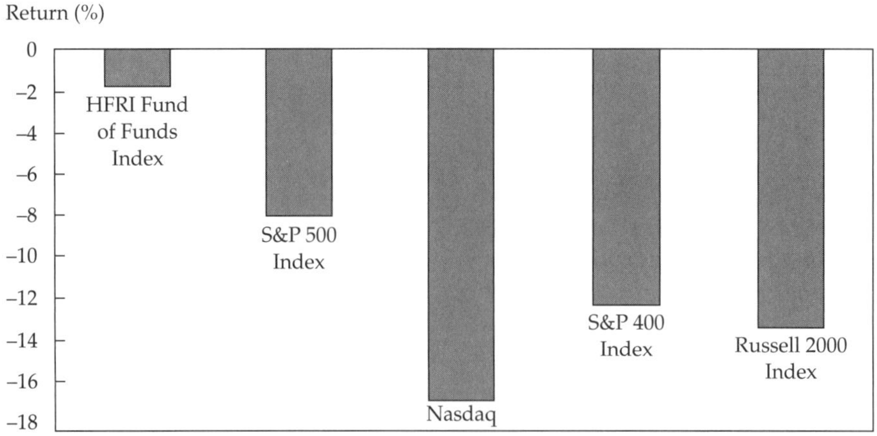

Index	Return (%)
HFRI Fund of Funds Index	approx. -1
S&P 500 Index	approx. -8
Nasdaq	approx. -17
S&P 400 Index	approx. -13
Russell 2000 Index	approx. -13

Source: Hedge Fund Research, Inc.

Who Invests in Hedge Funds?

Historically, high-net-worth investors have been the primary investors in hedge funds, but participation by other types of investors in this market is increasing. Institutional assets have been flowing in from pension funds, foundations and endowments, and not-for-profit organizations in particular. Nonetheless, about 75 percent of all capital invested in hedge funds is personal assets. In 1990, when the hedge fund industry was just getting off the ground, the industry was dominated by high-net-worth investors interested primarily in one thing—high performance. Expectations of a 40, 50, or 100 percent return from a hedge fund portfolio were not uncommon. By the mid-1990s, however, institutional money started to trickle into hedge funds as institutions started to become interested in diversifying away equity market risk. Thus, the reason most institutional investors had for investing in hedge funds was the exact opposite of that of high-net-worth individuals. The industry once dominated by investor expectations of incredibly high returns began to shift its focus to expectations of risk reduction through diversification.

Interestingly, the motivation for hedge fund investing by institutions has come full circle. Now, many pension funds are saying, "We can no longer meet our actuarial assumptions given the market's performance"; foundations and endowments are saying, "We cannot continue to fund our grants and cannot make our spending policies given the market's performance"; and high-net-worth investors are saying, "We cannot maintain our lifestyle given the market's performance." Therefore, the fundamental driver behind entry into hedge funds has returned to the goal of return generation, although with more moderate return expectations. In high-net-worth communities, for example, the return expectations for hedge funds have been ratcheted down considerably to 15–18 percent a year instead of 25–50 percent a year. At the same time, capital preservation has continued to be an important component of investors' interest in hedge funds.

Investment Structure

The investment structure of hedge funds is important because of the implications the various structures have for the fees the investor will pay, the control the investor can exert over the investment strategy, and the research and administrative responsibilities the investor will undertake. The high-net-worth market can invest in hedge funds in two ways: either directly or through a fund of funds. The institutional market can use the same two methods that individual investors can (direct investment and through a fund of funds), but institutional investors can also create a separately managed account for investing in hedge funds.

Direct Investment. Investing directly usually requires $1 million for each hedge fund in which the client invests; and that $1 million is generally locked up for at least one year. Liquidity after that first year can be quarterly, semiannual, or annual, but hedge funds are getting more restrictive as the asset class is becoming more popular.

The fee structure for hedge funds makes hedge fund management more expensive than for any other type of investment management vehicle. A hedge fund investor will pay, on average, a 1 percent management fee and an additional 20 percent of the profits to the hedge fund manager. The justification for the fee is that the managers use skill-based strategies that require them to use investment strategies that go beyond riding equity market waves and stock picking. On the one hand, with direct investment the investor has much greater control over the investment in terms of manager selection. But on the other hand, direct investment is research intensive and administratively burdensome, and the complex issue of manager cross-correlation can lower the anticipated risk reduction of hedge fund investing.

Fund of Funds. Investing through a fund of funds has several advantages. The first is the consolidation of information. A diversified hedge fund portfolio needs access to at least 10 funds. But investing in 10 funds comes with a high minimum price tag of $1 million each and an enormous administrative burden, namely, the receipt of 10 monthly performance reports, 10 quarterly commentaries, 10 annual K-1s, and 10 annual audits. So, for a family office, in particular, hedge fund diversity can carry a very high administrative cost. The same 10 funds bundled in a fund-of-funds program, however, significantly reduces the administrative burden for the investor, who then has only 1 instead of 10 of each of those documents. Thus, family offices that do not have a tremendous back-office staff typically choose the fund-of-funds route.

Another advantage of using a fund of funds comes from the fund-of-funds manager's ability to conduct research. New hedge fund managers seem to be appearing on the scene every day, and staying on top of all the new information in a timely fashion is difficult. Further confounding the problem is that the industry is unregulated and reporting by hedge funds is voluntary, so no centralized, trustworthy source of information exists for the universe of approximately 5,000 funds. As a consequence, at Northern Trust Global Investments, we recommend that individual investors without an institutional-type staff take the fund-of-funds route and pay the extra level of fees. In the fund-of-funds world, the investor pays the typical 1 percent management fee and 20 percent of profits to each underlying manager, but the investor also pays the fund-of-funds manager a 1 percent management fee on the total investment and 10 percent of the net profits of the fund of funds. Typically, the bottom-line fee to the investor is 2 percent of account value plus 30 percent of the profits.

Separately Managed Account. Institutional investors, primarily, can choose to hire a hedge fund manager to manage assets in a separate account that segregates the investor's assets from those of other investors. The investor can negotiate everything, including lockup provisions, fees, liquidity, and transparency. The problem is that separately managed accounts are extremely costly. Hedge fund managers these days are not willing to touch a separately managed account for anything less than a $10 million initial investment, and that minimum is increasing. (I have heard of minimums being as high as $50 million to $100 million.) And some managers simply refuse to run a separately managed account for a single investor, no matter the account size. Thus, the number of hedge fund managers willing to manage separate accounts is limited. Another drawback is that in a separately managed account, the investor has unlimited liability. For example, if an investor puts $10 million in a separately managed account, leverages it, and then all the shorts go the wrong way and the fund is down $20 million, the investor is on the hook for the $20 million to the prime broker. In contrast, under the limited partnership structure of a hedge fund, the investor's liability is limited.

Advisor Selection

High-net-worth investors, whether directly or through family offices, tend to choose investment managers via word of mouth. Thus, recommendations from family and friends who have had a positive experience with a hedge fund often outweigh the influence of research and due diligence in choosing a hedge fund for investment. This kind of referral-based decision making is prone to risks—risks that institutional investors are often familiar with but less-sophisticated individual investors are not.

One risk is that hedge fund managers sometimes give fee kickbacks to fund-of-funds managers or consultants. That is, the consultant says to the hedge fund manager, "I am going to put my client's $10 million in your fund, but I want you to kick back to me some portion of that fee." The first question an investor should ask any consultant or fund-of-funds manager even before discussing performance expectations is whether he or she accepts fee rebates. The answer is almost always going to be "no" because managers know better. The more important and relevant question is whether any of their affiliates do. What happens time and time again is that a consultant or a fund-of-funds manager says to a client, "I am a registered investment advisor; I am not going to take kickbacks," but the consultant or fund-of-funds manager may own an affiliated broker/dealer or a third-party marketing firm that may engage in rebating.

Investors want to be sure their consultants or fund-of-funds managers have no inherent conflicts of interest. The fear, of course, is that if fee-sharing arrangements exist between managers and consultants or between managers and fund-of-funds managers, then the likelihood is reduced that a "preferred" manager will be fired by the consultant or fund-of-funds manager. And if such an arrangement does exist, then the consultant or fund-of-funds manager will likely recommend funds only from this limited universe of hedge fund managers. Therefore, investors need to find out whether the rebate from the hedge fund manager is voluntary or mandatory. If it is mandatory, then investors should be concerned about limiting their subfund universe because of the relationship between their fund-of-funds managers and the subfund managers. But the fact that a consultant or fund-of-funds manager gets a rebate is not always cause for concern. Sometimes the fund-of-funds manager will give the rebate to the client. If the consultant's or fund-of-funds manager's clients are fee sensitive, then this arrangement can be advantageous to both the consultant and client.

Manager platforms are a relatively new structure and come with their own risks. In a manager platform, a consultant creates a menu of hedge funds by hiring a stable of managers. The advantage is that these managers are managing the hedge fund assets within separately managed accounts. The excitement surrounding separately managed accounts is that they are viewed as the only fraud-proof structure that can be created; they are the only structure in which a hedge fund manager cannot abscond with the money. So, the selling point for these manager platforms is that the investor can hire 15 managers and have each of them run a separately managed account, an advantage that gives the investor some assurance the managers will not commit fraud.

Manager platforms nevertheless have some inherent problems. One problem is that separately managed accounts have unlimited liability, as I discussed earlier. Another problem is getting high-quality managers onto the manager platform. To get a hedge fund manager to run a separately managed account is like pulling teeth. I mentioned earlier that minimums for separately managed accounts can be as high as $50 million to $100 million, but most of these manager platforms are promising managers small dollars up front—$2 million to $5 million. Thus, many of these platforms may have substandard managers because the better ones will not participate.

A final source of concern is that manager platforms often involve a fee-sharing arrangement because the way the manager-platform provider gets paid is through the underlying manager fees. These programs seem attractive because the manager-platform providers are touting a fund of funds in a virtually fraud-proof structure that saves the investor from paying the double layer of fees associated with a traditional fund of funds. But any time a lot of people are involved in a cooperative hedge fund effort—people who all need to get paid—investors should start asking questions.

Another risk investors need to be advised of is the risk that comes from hedge fund incubators. Established investment management firms are buying start-up hedge funds because the new hedge funds are seen as being better able to generate performance than many older hedge funds that have grown very large. The new, smaller funds promise more trading flexibility—viewed as contributing to better performance. So, a number of firms are taking equity stakes in emerging funds, incubating them, adding them to their infrastructure, and then taking a percentage of their profits. This business model is not all bad, but again, it does create conflicts of interest. Therefore, when advisors are seeking and recommending hedge funds for their clients, they want to make sure they understand any incubator or seed capital relationship a fund may have.

Benchmark Selection

Benchmarking in hedge fund investing can be confusing. A hedge fund portfolio can be benchmarked in a number of ways. One way to benchmark a fund, which can be viewed as a cop-out given the high-fee structure of hedge funds, is to use a positive return—whereby a hedge fund manager benchmarks to any return above zero. The second and more common way is to use an absolute return—a quantified, predetermined percentage year in and year out. So, a 15 percent absolute return means the manager targets a 15 percent return, regardless of the market environment. Using an absolute return is standard for a fund of funds, but using an absolute return is more difficult for managers of a single fund because all hedge fund strategies are subject to short-term cycles that cause the strategy to move in and out of positive-return territory; thus, achieving a fixed-percentage positive return every year is difficult for these funds. Another alternative is relative returns—returns relative to hedge fund indexes, various strategy indexes, peer groups, and, of course, the market.

Investors should beware of a hedge fund manager who claims to benchmark to an absolute return but whose biggest graph on the monthly performance report shows the manager's performance versus the S&P 500. Of course, when managers beat the S&P 500, they want to talk about it. But such discussions put investors in a relative benchmarking mode when, in fact, they may have invested because of absolute return potential. This switch to relative benchmarking is particularly a problem in the high-net-worth market. Most institutional investors have concrete expectations that do not waiver. But, in the high-net-worth world, investors are generally satisfied as long as they are getting a better return than they would somewhere else. Thus, investors should clearly articulate their performance goals in advance because if their benchmark differs from their manager's, the relationship will not be satisfactory over a long period of time. And if the investor's and manager's benchmarks are in conflict, the investor should find another manager whose benchmark is consistent with the investor's. In the long run, investors are more likely to be happy in a hedge fund investment if their goals are well defined and do not change substantially over time.

Strategy Selection

Strategy selection can also be a source of risk for investors. **Figure 2** shows the risk and return profile for the HFRI Fund Weighted Composite Index (indicated by a circle); various market indexes (indicated by triangles), such as the Lehman Brothers Aggregate Bond Index and the S&P 500; and various hedge fund strategies (indicated by squares). Compared with all the indexes shown in Figure 2, the HFRI Fund Weighted Composite Index had superior risk-adjusted returns. That is, during the past 12 years, the hedge fund index's returns, while beating those of the S&P 500, had about half of the volatility of the S&P 500 returns.

One point worth noting in Figure 2 is the sheer number and breadth of hedge fund strategies. Most investors automatically think of George Soros, Julian Robertson, or Long-Term Capital Management (LTCM) when they think of hedge funds, but all of those strategies would have been to the far right on the directional side. In reality, the majority of hedge fund dollars are invested in more market-neutral approaches that are closer to the left side of the figure (i.e., the low-risk and low-to-moderate return strategies). Most of the hedge fund strategies fall nearer to the Lehman Brothers Aggregate Bond Index than to the opposite side of the spectrum on the risk–reward scale.

The market-neutral area of Figure 2 contains strategies that generate returns uncorrelated to the equity markets and strategies that have been sufficiently hedged to insulate market movements. For

Figure 2. Risk versus Reward for Various Hedge Fund Strategies and Market Indexes, 1990–2001

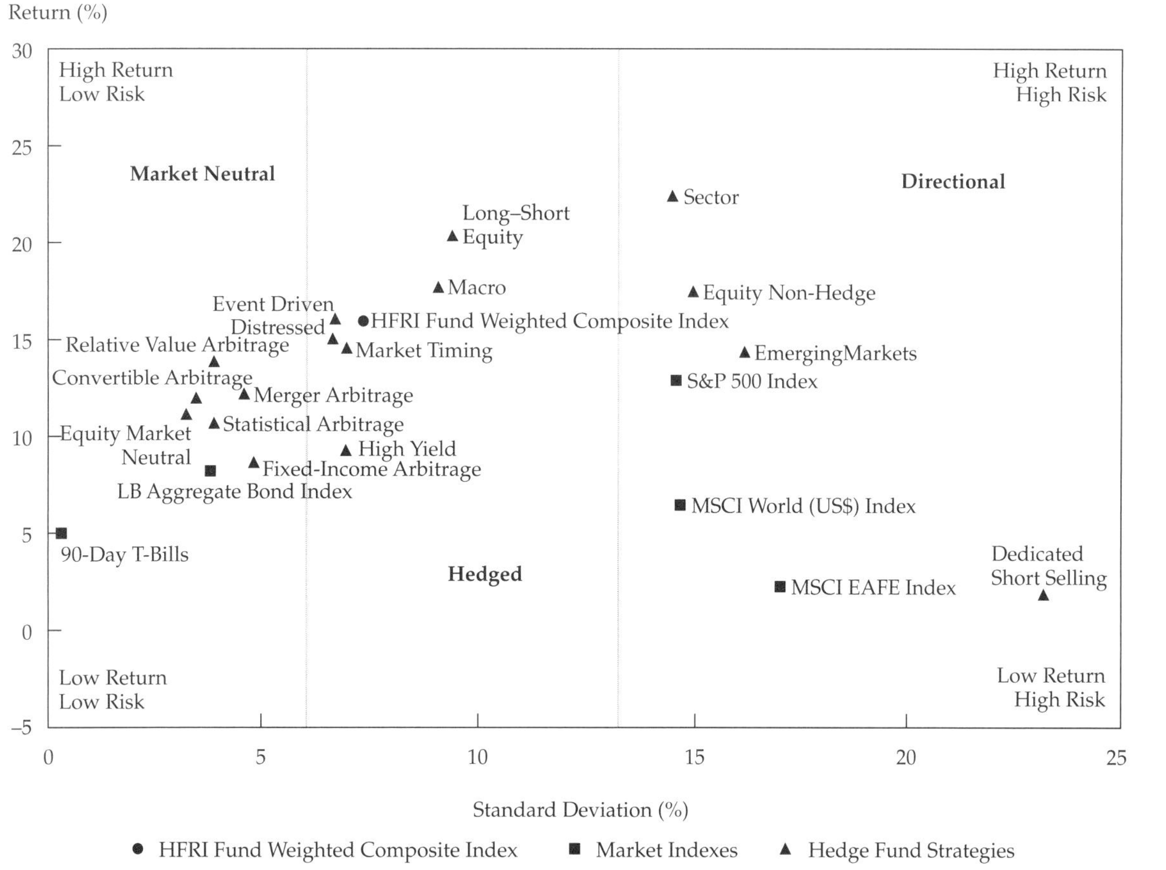

Note: Returns shown are average monthly returns, net of fees.
Source: Hedge Fund Research, Inc.

example, in convertible arbitrage, the manager is long the convertible bond and short the underlying stock; such a strategy is viewed as market neutral because the source of return has nothing to do with the behavior of the equity market. For equity-based strategies, such as statistical arbitrage, dollar neutrality across the long and short sides is maintained. In the hedged area, long–short equity is probably the most popular style. In this strategy, the manager has downside protection, but the portfolio is not necessarily fully hedged; it has some directionality. And finally, the directional area contains the strategies in which a great deal of directionality comes into play, such as dedicated short selling. Moving from the bottom left to the top right of the figure, the upside potential of the strategy increases, but the downside potential increases as well.

One of the biggest changes in the past three or four years in hedge fund investing is the increased risk of the likelihood of underperformance unless investors are invested broadly across hedge fund strategies. Three years ago, if a client wanted to target a 15 percent annual return in his or her hedge fund investments, the probability was high that the advisor would have concentrated on just a handful of strategy bets in selecting the hedge fund portfolio. Certainly, the advisor would have diversified to some degree, but the advisor would have thought that the likelihood of getting two or three strategy bets right was pretty good. Successful multiple-manager programs three or four years ago often consisted of perhaps five different strategies among 8 or 10 hedge fund managers. So, if the advisor picked the correct strategy bets, those bets would provide a tremendous amount of upside potential to the portfolio. And investing broadly across multiple strategies and managers at that time would have, in all likelihood, diversified out some of the upside for the portfolio.

That situation has completely changed. Today, hedge fund strategies are subject to compressed short-term strategy cycles, much like the equity markets. So, the probability of positive returns over a long time period is much greater now than ever before *if* the investor's portfolio is more broadly diversified. But how an advisor and a fund-of-funds manager accomplish that diversification differs. Say an advisor needs to invest a client's $15 million portfolio and in the interest of breadth chooses 15 hedge funds to invest in directly. The advisor would likely view each independently and pick 15 good funds. A fund-of-funds manager, however, would view the 15 funds in terms of a totality, not individually. The "net" view of fund-of-funds managers creates a radically different investment program than that created by an advisor. For example, the short-selling strategy shown in Figure 2 had about twice the volatility of the S&P 500, with a return of about 0.2 percent for the 12-year period. Chances are that an advisor would not select a dedicated short seller because this strategy would probably lose money 10 out of 12 months. The fund-of-funds manager is also familiar with the high-loss probability of a dedicated short seller, but the tremendous positive return that a short seller can contribute in periods of severe market decline mitigates that downside risk. The fund-of-funds manager is, therefore, willing to use the short seller as an insurance policy. Although the advisor can use the dedicated short seller in the same fashion, because each fund's performance is reported individually to the client, client reaction to continual losses may inhibit the advisor's willingness to embrace a holistic strategy similar to the fund-of-funds manager's approach.

Manager Selection

When investors are trying to select a hedge fund manager, they must consider their own research methods, the risks of investing with a particular manager, and the amount of disclosure a manager provides. By focusing on these issues, investors will be better able to make informed decisions.

Research Methodology. In the high-net-worth world, I cannot overemphasize the risks of word-of-mouth "research." Historically, the hedge fund industry has been secretive and protective, and an individual's ability to find complete information is limited and the process expensive. As a result, family offices and individuals tend to select hedge funds by word of mouth. For example, Michael Berger's Manhattan Investment Fund and LTCM—funds that failed and whose clients lost everything—are examples of hedge funds whose clients invested in them primarily through referrals by friends and family. In the case of the Manhattan Investment Fund, Michael Berger started committing fraud in 1997, but it was not discovered until 2000, even though the fund was audited every year during that period.

Large investors usually outsource the research function to fund-of-funds managers or consultants to avoid the risks associated with incomplete managerial due diligence. Access to industrywide sources is improving, but only those advisors and consultants who work with hedge funds on a full-time basis have sufficient knowledge in this complex industry.

Risks of Investing. Investors who are drawn to alternative investment strategies because of their potential returns face a dilemma: Hedge fund strategies can reduce overall portfolio risk, but accessing these strategies can increase other risks in the portfolio, risks that are not found in the traditional investment management world. By investing in hedge funds, investors face the risks associated with derivatives, short selling, and leverage. And additionally, they face the risks of the hedge fund manager misrepresenting the investments in his or her fund, changing his or her investment style (or experiencing style drift), and committing fraud or making an incorrect valuation. With no other asset class is the phrase "past performance is not indicative of future returns" more applicable than with hedge funds. The two main risks for clients who choose to invest in hedge fund strategies are leverage and manipulated valuations.

Leverage. Leverage can be dangerous to use. For every dollar LTCM invested, it had $100 exposed to the market (leveraged 100:1), and the overextended fund quickly unraveled as a result. Nonetheless, although the use of leverage may seem scary to investors, leverage does have two often overlooked benefits. First, some hedge fund strategies would not be at all attractive without leverage. With fixed-income arbitrage, for example, the spreads are so small that there is no reason to invest unless the manager leverages the positions. Leverage ranging from 8:1 to 15:1 is normal in fixed-income arbitrage and is not viewed as risky but, rather, as an integral and necessary part of the investment strategy. When looking at hedge fund managers, investors thus need to keep in mind the strategy the manager uses before asking about the leverage level because a positive relationship may exist between the two.

Some managers also use leverage to hedge. When screening hedge funds, if an investor finds that a hedge fund manager's leverage is high, the investor should investigate further. For example, some long–short equity managers use leverage only to put on pairs trades or shorts because they like their longs. They are confident their longs will increase in value, and the only way they can afford to put on more downside protection is to sell those favorable long positions or leverage the portfolio. In many cases, managers use leverage to reduce risk as opposed to increasing return, which is the purpose most people normally associate with leverage.

Valuation. The second risk in terms of accessing the hedge fund industry is valuation. All of the hedge fund frauds that have been widely reported in the news happened essentially the same way. The hedge fund manager had losses in the portfolio but reported falsified positive returns to the investors. The manager then leveraged the portfolio to try to make the money back, continued to lose money, and still reported positive returns to investors. Such a scheme eventually collapses, but until it does, even though nothing is left in the fund, investors think they have had a fabulous year because of the fudged valuations reported by the fund.

Avoiding that kind of fraud is difficult, but it is possible to "structure out" the ability to commit fraud. With a separately managed account, the investor can see the positions and verify the reported returns. But that analysis requires the ability to independently value the securities, which is difficult for the high-net-worth investor. Institutions normally outsource this function, sometimes to a third-party administrator or a fund-of-funds manager, and each security is repriced by an independent source. Independent valuation is the only way an investor can make certain the return reported by the manager is accurate.

In the absence of a separately managed account, the likelihood that a hedge fund manager will give a high-net-worth investor access to the fund's positions is negligible. The reason hedge fund managers give for this secrecy is that they do not want investors to reverse engineer their portfolios (and if anybody truly has the ability to do that, I would love to see it). The reality is that hedge fund managers do not want to answer 499 telephone calls from their investors asking, "Hey, why are you in Enron?" The desire to limit investors' microlevel questions about the fund's positions is what really drives the lack of disclosure to the high-net-worth market. The institutional market is a little different, however. Ideally, institutional investors have an arrangement with the fund manager—an arrangement that contains a strict confidentiality agreement—that allows them access to the fund's positions because hedge fund managers understand that institutional clients will not invest in a fund without adequate transparency.

Disclosure. Although the norm is for institutional investors to have better access to information on a fund's positions than high-net-worth investors, high-net-worth investors should never discount their right to transparency and should only invest in those funds that offer a level of disclosure that makes them comfortable. I know a high-net-worth client that has been invested in a hedge fund for seven years and is completely happy. I asked the client what the fund's investment strategy was, not which stocks the fund holds, and this client had no idea. If an investor is comfortable with little or no information, then such flexibility gives an investor a large universe of hedge funds to buy. But if a private investor requires more disclosure, then the field may be markedly narrowed. Given the fact that between 4,000 and 6,000 funds exist, investors should be able to find a manager with a strategy that complements their investment goals and that will provide the level of disclosure they demand.

I also suggest that clients shop around when looking for a hedge fund manager. If a client of mine is absolutely convinced a particular manager is the right one, I tell her to ask that manager which of her competitors most closely resembles her investment style. Invariably, the manager will mention a fund manager who is equally fabulous and who uses the same strategy. I then tell my client to go visit this other manager and see whether she is still as impressed with the first manager. Oftentimes, the client's opinion will change.

Industry Trends

Keeping pace with recent industry trends, such as rapidly increasing fees and greater liquidity restrictions, is critical for high-net-worth investors. For example, a recently launched fund of funds charges, in addition to the underlying fund manager fees, a 1.5 percent management fee, a 1.25 percent administrative fee, and 10 percent of the profits. It also has a four-year lockup. For any withdrawals prior to the four-year lockup expiration, a 5 percent redemption fee is assessed. The cost of gaining access to hedge fund strategies is much more expensive than it used to be. At the same time, lockups are getting longer. A major bank is launching a fund-of-funds program that has a seven-year lockup, which resembles a private equity liquidity term. Investors will continue to see lockup periods lengthen.

Another industry trend is a revisiting of the reliability of audits. Considering the example of the Manhattan Investment Fund, whose false returns had been audited but went undetected, investors need to find clever ways to independently value portfolios, which is extremely difficult. One alternative is for the investor to try to get information about the top 10 positions in the fund on a monthly basis. If the manager will share that information, the investor can do rational price checking. Say a merger arbitrage manager tells an investor that the fund is up 5 percent for the month of March 2002, but if the fund's top 10 positions include the General Electric Company, Honeywell International, and Enron Corporation, the investor knows that the 5 percent return is incorrect. Although the investor has enough information to question the manager's reported return, the investor's information is still incomplete.

The attempt to structurally eliminate fraud by using separately managed accounts continues. Unfortunately, separately managed accounts are too expensive for individual investors and smaller institutional investors to use and too administratively complicated for hedge fund managers to want to manage. Separately managed accounts may be suitable for large institutional investors, such as CalPERS (California Public Employees' Retirement System), but for most investors, separately managed accounts require additional staff and time because of individualized accounting and back-office procedures. Therefore, separately managed accounts will remain rare, particularly for the high-net-worth investor.

On the upside, manager disclosure to investors has improved significantly as a direct result of institutional assets entering the marketplace. High-net-worth investors have been able to take advantage of this trend. Hedge fund investors (individual as well as institutional) are receiving more informative quarterly commentary and monthly disclosure letters than ever before, and this trend should continue.

Finally, returns are becoming, at least for now, more dependent on diversification than ever before. If the market turns strongly bullish, this situation will change. But for the time being, in order to structure a successful ongoing hedge fund investment program, investors will have to seek a greater degree of diversification than they would have three or four years ago.

Conclusion

Hedge funds are becoming a mainstream asset class among high-net-worth investors. Previously, only the ultra wealthy dabbled in this area, but now, investors with as little as $1 million in net worth are investing in hedge funds. Hedge funds are experiencing a moderate expansion into the retail marketplace, and some funds are even becoming registered so that they can accept investors from the general public. Hedge fund investing, however, has risks unlike those in any other sector of the market. Investors have to juggle the trade-off between their desire to earn positive returns in bear markets and how much they are willing to accept in terms of risk. As long as investors can maintain a suitable balance between the rewards and risks of hedge funds, hedge funds can be an interesting investment choice.

Question and Answer Session
Lori R. Runquist

Question: Most hedge funds generate large short-term gains. Please address their after-tax performance.

Runquist: Hedge funds are inherently tax inefficient and always will be. Tax inefficiency can be handled a couple of ways, but some flexibility is lost in the process. The only ways I know to reduce tax inefficiency are to use long-term insurance wrappers and structured products.

On the structured-product side, an investment bank invests on behalf of the taxable client, but the arrangement cannot look like a tax shelter. It has to look like a leveraging instrument. The advisor brings $1 million of his client's money to an institution that, in turn, extends $5 million to a hedge fund. The trade-off is the lockup period. Normally, these vehicles have a liquidity provision that says the investor cannot touch the invested capital for about five years. Because one of the most attractive things about hedge fund investing is the liquidity, the problem with using structured products for hedge fund investing, given the inherent risk of an unregulated environment, is that the investor has to give up liquidity on a quarterly, semiannual, or annual basis.

Weighing tax efficiency against the loss of liquidity is tricky. The issue of taxes used to be a more prevalent concern for high-net-worth clients, but based on what I have been hearing during the past year or so, a tax-inefficient positive return is preferable to a negative return, although I do not know how long that attitude will last.

Question: How much of a typical high-net-worth client's portfolio do you recommend putting in hedge funds?

Runquist: The industry standard is about 10 percent, but the answer depends on the investor's level of comfort and experience. Many investors have as much as 70 percent in nothing but alternative investments, and I know some who have nothing but hedge funds and private equity in their portfolios. At Northern Trust, we think 10 percent is a smart place to start; any amount less than that may not be enough to offset the equity risk in the investor's overall portfolio.

For first-time investors, however, we suggest starting smaller, and the wealthier the client, the smaller the percentage of total assets. We usually recommend that clients with $50 million to $100 million in assets begin with an initial investment in hedge funds of 5, 6, or 7 percent and then build on that allocation.

Question: How does the 1997 repeal of short positions in mutual funds change the relative advantage of hedge funds?

Runquist: The majority of hedge fund strategies, not counting long–short equity, are strategies in which the source of return is derived from something other than stock picking. For hedge funds that use merger activity in their strategy, for example, their source of return is derived solely from the closing of the deal. In fixed-income arbitrage, distressed debt, or any of the other arbitrage strategies, the source of return derives from capturing a spread. Thus, the ability of mutual funds to short stocks has no impact on these investment approaches.

With long–short equity, however, the answer is twofold. First, mutual fund managers who are allowed to short are restricted in the amount they can short, so these managers have limited flexibility. I believe the restriction is that only 25 percent of the portfolio can be invested in shorts. In the long–short equity universe, the hedge fund return for September 2001 was as strong as it was because hedge fund managers had the flexibility to go completely net short, and many of them did. Second, it is the ability to turn on a dime in choppy markets and to go net short or completely to cash that gives hedge funds their advantage in down markets. The mutual fund industry simply does not have that flexibility yet.

Question: The HFRI performance indexes have always looked terrific on a risk–return basis, but aren't they uninvestable and subject to a self-reporting bias?

Runquist: Unfortunately, no good index for hedge funds exists, and reporting is voluntary. Furthermore, from an analytical standpoint, all hedge fund indexes consist of leveraged and unleveraged funds. They also consist of domestic and offshore funds. If George Soros has one giant fund composed of an onshore feeder and an offshore feeder and they do exactly the same thing, Soros will turn in two numbers at the end of the month because he has two separate legal entities. So, the complexity of problems surrounding hedge fund indexes is enormous.

As long as hedge funds remain an unregulated industry that the average retail client cannot enter, we will have imperfect measurement.

Regarding the question of investable indexes, the problem in the hedge fund world is defining the universe. Suppose you want to create an index for merger arbitrage. How do you define the universe of merger arbitrage? It is not the S&P 500. You cannot just pick the number of stocks that are available. Do you, for example, look at all the merger arbitrage managers that will give you information and then try to fund weight the different deals in proportion to what they hold? Or is the index just one share of every available deal? Such complexity will always be a part of investable indexes in the hedge fund universe because the universes cannot be clearly defined.

This lack of an investable universe means that for performance measurement we use hedge fund indexes differently from the way a traditional manager would use a traditional index because we have no other choice. Normally, we take a broad-based overview of peer-group performance at the substrategy and fund-of-funds levels and little else. I am hesitant to use the HFRI Fund Weighted Composite Index for performance measurement because, among other things, it includes strategies and managers that practice investment approaches beyond our clients' risk tolerance. Furthermore, no index measures more than 12 years of data.

When investors are thinking about making a first-time allocation to hedge fund programs, we thus caution them about relying too heavily on past performance at the index level because of all the complexities of the indexes. The trick is to figure out, from an investment standpoint, which strategies appear to have return opportunities and which ones have risks the investor wants to avoid.

Question: Returns for most hedge fund strategies have been lower in the past 12–18 months than they have been historically. Is too much money chasing hedge fund strategies?

Runquist: There are a couple things to keep in mind about the returns of hedge funds. The first is that hedge fund strategies, by and large, use publicly traded securities. Because hedge funds are worth about $500 billion, they constitute about 0.5 percent of all the money in the capital markets.

The problem is that the volatile markets of the past 18 months have affected strategies in weird ways. For example, mergers have taken a hit. Deals are falling apart not because there is too much money in merger arbitrage but because of what is going on in the corporate marketplace. In 2001, we saw a new risk to merger arbitrage; deals were breaking up because of negative surprise earnings announcements. Deals used to break up because of regulatory or antitrust concerns, but now, stock market volatility is affecting company valuations and the closing of deals.

We also saw problems in long–short equity because every other day, the drivers of the economy, both old economy and new economy companies, were getting whipsawed around. The hedge fund managers, much like the mutual fund managers, had a difficult time navigating their way through that environment.

So, no, I do not think the reduction in hedge fund returns has to do with too much money chasing the funds. It is an interesting question, however, because historically, money has always been chasing "the hot strategy." About three years ago, mergers closed every day and were fabulously profitable. A lot of investment money went to merger arbitrage, and everybody and their brother launched a merger arbitrage fund. But now, the merger deals have dried up, and all the money is racing to distressed debt. The distressed-debt managers are excited, saying that they are not to capacity yet, supply outreaches demand, and so on. There are issues of capacity, but we are not at all saturated at this point.

Also keep in mind that as misevaluations occur in the marketplace, somebody will be smart enough to capitalize on them, and it will be a hedge fund manager with a strategy no one has yet seen. For example, this year hedge fund merger arbitrage managers came up with a new twist on their strategy. When the mergers started to dry up, some managers shifted their strategy to shorting deals they thought would break. For smart managers, hedge funds offer infinite flexibility. Given the fact that the market will always be mispriced in some sense, money-making opportunities will always be around. It is just a question of how many hedge fund managers will be able to do it well.

Question: What type of transparency does a fund-of-funds manager have?

Runquist: The answer depends on what the fund-of-funds manager wants and expects and what he can do about it. One thing to note is that transparency is only as good as the exit strategy. If a fund-of-funds manager notices a manager of an individual hedge fund experiencing strategy drift or marking up returns but the fund-of-funds manager cannot get his clients' capital out for a year or two, what good does it do? Even with perfect transparency, advisors should always ask what the fund-of-funds manager can do if something goes wrong. Some options are available. The fund-of-funds manager can negotiate up-front contracts with underlying hedge fund managers for early exit clauses or rescissions if managers violate material provisions.

Fund-of-funds managers' attitudes on transparency fall into one of two camps, depending on their comfort zone. The first camp I call the "old school," which consists of privately owned or previously privately owned fund-of-funds boutiques, such as Grosvenor Funds and Blackstone Group. This first camp, by and large, will manufacture fund-of-funds programs with the rationale that the investor should invest in them because the programs have access to "all the good funds that are closed." Most of these fund of funds are older. This group is not getting much, if any, disclosure from these underlying managers because the managers in this camp have chosen to invest in funds that they think will generate good performance but that also have a history of being somewhat secretive.

Camp number two is a newer group in which an institutional attitude about transparency is evident. Normally, the managers in this camp are institutional players, such as the Northern Trust, the Goldman Sachs Group, Morgan Stanley Dean Witter & Company, and J.P. Morgan Chase & Company, which primarily have institutional clients with different expectations from those of the clients in the first camp. Most of these fund-of-funds will be given some degree of transparency to the underlying funds. The trade-off is that the majority of these programs are considerably younger than those in the first group.

The challenge as an investor, then, is to figure out which level of transparency is comfortable and to weigh that against the importance of past performance.

Managing Performance: Monitoring and Transitioning Managers

Louisa W. Sellers
Managing Director
Ashbridge Investment Management, LLC
Philadelphia

> The due diligence associated with manager selection is critically important, particularly for the selection of hedge fund managers and managers of taxable portfolios and when transitioning from one manager to another. Thus, the tools and methods used to select managers and monitor the managers' adherence to the style for which they were selected are vital. The crucial elements in a manager's ability to maintain investment style over time are performance, continuity of personnel, conformity to style, and consistency in procedures.

Ashbridge Investment Management originated as the family office for the Grace family, whose wealth was created by Bethlehem Steel Corporation. The Grace family has been through several iterations of managing its wealth, the latest of which began a little more than 20 years ago. This most recent iteration involved a series of decisions by the family that included establishing an investment policy, setting an asset allocation, and hiring outside managers to fulfill the investment mandates. Such an approach does not seem that unusual today; however, for a family to have embarked in this direction 20 years ago is somewhat unique. Although pension plans, endowments, and universities had begun to follow this model, most families at that time were investing primarily in large-cap stocks and municipal bonds.

The Grace family's foresight resulted in the organization of Ashbridge Investment Management. At Ashbridge, we now serve about 40 families and clients in addition to the Grace family. The firm's growth has greatly expanded our knowledge base, thus enabling us to increase the number of asset classes and strategies we can make available within our established allocations. We currently allocate to about 60 different managers that span about 25 different asset classes and strategies. The asset classes and strategies we use are domestic and international, long only, and alternative. By alternative, I mean predominately hedged strategies as opposed to private equity and venture capital.

In the course of my presentation, I will touch on a variety of topics, from what it means to monitor managers in general, and hedge fund managers in particular (because hedge fund management is more complex than long-only strategies), to exchange-traded funds (ETFs) and tax-efficient investing.

Background

The initial due diligence involved in selecting managers is crucial, but perhaps even more important is the ongoing due diligence of managers once they are selected, particularly in the open architecture model that prevails in the marketplace today. Every investment management firm, no matter whether it is a large investment bank or a trust company, seems to realize that even though a lot of approaches to investing can be successful, no single firm can be an expert in all of them.

Many variations exist for the open architecture model. For Ashbridge, it simply means working as a consultant on behalf of the client and sitting on the client's side of the table. We outsource all custodial and managerial work but retain in-house the setting of policy and the reporting on the outcome of that policy. Our concept of open architecture necessitates extensive discussions between the consultant and the family about the family's long-term and short-term objectives for its wealth. For example, allocating across various investment pockets within the family means establishing asset allocations for family limited partnerships, generation-skipping trusts, charitable trusts, and foundations. The entire plan must be synthesized in a reasonable way.

We set asset allocations for a family's total assets as well as for the individual entities within the family structure and then seek managers to fulfill those allocations. Through our manager selection, we try to create a style, market-capitalization, geographical, and strategy blend that includes hedged strategies to control risk.

Selecting an Investment Manager

The initial due diligence on a manager is exhaustive. Typically, the process begins with a database search that has a quantitative focus. A consultant can subscribe to a number of different services that will find thousands of managers around the world. Manager performance is an important factor at this stage, but the performance and the period over which performance is calculated is merely the initial qualifier. We evaluate each manager over a three-year horizon because we want to see how the manager has performed in different markets and how the performance averages out over time.

This screen of the databases provides a subset of managers that is about 20 percent of the original manager universe, which we then evaluate qualitatively. Our qualitative analysis involves fairly rigorous fundamental analysis followed by face-to-face discussions. We rely on one or more face-to-face meetings to solidify what we have learned previously through the quantitative data, telephone conversations, and conference calls. Our goal is to meet the portfolio manager and to ensure adequate access to him or her during our ongoing monitoring of that manager. The chemistry between the portfolio manager and the trader is also an important variable in our decision-making process, especially if their interaction is a key component to the strategy we are using. Furthermore, we want to become acquainted with the analysts at the firm and determine who our primary contact will be; if it is a client services person, we try to find out how knowledgeable that person is about the firm and the execution of the firm's strategy.

Many questions need to be asked throughout the manager-selection process, which can take 6–24 months, depending on the manager and the strategy. We prefer to act slowly and perhaps forgo some return to prepare ourselves for a relationship with a manager. Our goal is to be confident in our decision because we do not want to have to terminate a manager. Certain managers have been working with us for more than 10 years, which demonstrates the importance of doing excellent work at the outset, during the search stage. We believe our efforts will ultimately improve the returns of our clients' portfolios at a reasonable level of risk.

Monitoring an Investment Manager

The ongoing due diligence of managers we have hired has a slightly different character from the initial due diligence in a manager search, but it nevertheless entails the same quantitative and qualitative criteria used in selecting managers. On an ongoing basis, however, our most important concern is to make sure the manager's strategy is being executed as expected. This oversight builds confidence in the managers we have hired and, in turn, allows us to convey that comfort and confidence to our clients. Furthermore, monitoring managers on an ongoing basis reduces risk by identifying style drift or organizational changes early, before any performance deterioration. We cover four areas in our ongoing due diligence process: performance, continuity, conformity to investment strategy, and consistency of procedures.

Performance. The first variable we review on an ongoing basis is performance. Performance tells the story right up front and clearly sets the tone of the exchange between the consultant and the manager before a conversation even begins. We focus on how the performance looks relative to style benchmarks, peer groups, and the market. Granted, choosing an appropriate performance benchmark is difficult, but for long-only strategies, thanks to the Frank Russell Company, Barra, and other benchmark providers, we have multiple ways to slice and dice almost every manager's portfolio according to market capitalization, style, geography, and sector.

Continuity. We also monitor continuity in personnel. Just as clients seek continuity in their advisors, we seek continuity in the personnel and structure of the manager's organization.

Conformity. Sometimes change is a good thing, but not for a manager given a specific mandate. Therefore, we review conformity to the style or strategy the manager was hired to execute. The manager's strategy is only one piece of a larger policy, so if the manager deviates significantly from his or her initial mandate, that deviation may cause problems.

Consistency. The final variable we monitor is the consistency of various procedures. Specifically, our concern centers on the manager's buy and sell disciplines.

Tools and Practices for Monitoring. To prepare for the monitoring process, we use a rigorous questionnaire that we develop for each manager. A questionnaire for a hedge fund manager, for example, requires that the manager answer as many as 125 questions. The questionnaire is followed by in-depth biographies of the individuals involved with the firm; information on the outside organizations that provide accounting, prime brokerage, and legal services to the manager; a statement about the amount of assets under management at the firm; and an explanation about the way the manager has grown or changed over time. All of the information we gather is gradually streamlined as the ongoing due diligence process is carried out; typically, "ongoing" means a quarterly interview, generally 10–20 days after the end of the calendar quarter. Additionally, we do onsite visits at least once a year.

The quarterly interviews are usually conducted via conference calls. For each call, we generally include a team of individuals with different backgrounds and skill sets to ensure that a wide variety of questions are asked and to broaden the scope of the material we want to cover with the manager. We primarily discuss the manager's most recent performance. If the manager's performance has deviated from his or her benchmark, particularly if it has deviated for the second or third quarter in a row, we view this trend as a problem. Obviously, defending his or her performance is a challenging position for the manager, but defending the manager's performance to the client is equally challenging for us.

Keep in mind that we adopt the role of the intermediary between the manager and the client in order to unearth any relevant issues. Often, the manager's performance turns around. As long as we are satisfied that the underperformance was a result of rational decision making, we will stay with the manager. Recommending to a client that a manager be terminated is not a decision we make lightly. Although a foundation, endowment, or other tax-exempt entity can change managers easily by simply liquidating assets and moving on, as I will discuss in the last section, for taxable clients, the decision to change managers is not as simple.

Once we have conducted our quarterly conference calls to each manager, all 60 of them, we record these interviews not only for our own use but also for the benefit of our clients. Each participant in the call records what he or she heard during the manager interview. Although everyone hears the same conversation, each person assigns a slightly different meaning to the same information; we like to compare the varying nuances arising from multiple points of view. Our conference call notes are synthesized to document the call and are then reported to clients as part of a comprehensive reporting package.

Onsite visits are a critical element in the ongoing due diligence process, just as they are in the initial manager search process. We make onsite visits to managers to assess the atmosphere of the firm and the chemistry between the portfolio managers, analysts, and traders.

Monitoring Hedge Funds. Monitoring a hedge fund manager is equivalent, in my view, to turbocharged monitoring of a long-only manager. An even deeper analysis must be done to understand a hedge fund manager's strategy and the execution of that strategy for a variety of reasons, including the lack of transparency of the portfolio, use of leverage, use of index futures and options, investment in illiquid securities, and tendency of the fund's beta to drift quite high.

A hedge fund's use of leverage and derivatives, combined with the lack of transparency, vastly increases the potential risks in a hedge fund's portfolio. And without sufficient transparency, the ability to satisfactorily assess these risks is seriously impaired. Some of the portfolio risks that concern us are a fund's counterparty risk, regulatory issues that could hamper the fund's strategy, security and credit concentrations, nonmarket security evaluations, currency exposure, and how well hedged the portfolio actually is. Typically, when we conduct a monitoring interview with a hedge fund manager, we ask questions that go far beyond what the manager's top-10 long holdings are. We want to know the manager's gross long and gross short exposures and how those exposures drive the manager to his or her net exposure. We also want to know the manager's top sector and geographical exposures, particularly if the manager is an international manager. Finally, we request that the fund disclose any potential liquidity considerations, especially on the fund's short positions.

Liquidity posed a particular problem a few years ago, when funds were stuffed with hot initial public offering (IPO) issues. Tremendous opportunity existed in 2000 to short many of the IPOs issued in 1998 and 1999, and as the IPO prices dropped, the short squeezes that resulted affected valuations. Most hedge fund managers will not disclose their short positions; they will divulge their sector or country exposure on the short side or the total short exposure in the portfolio, but rarely will they divulge the names of their short stocks. Also, knowing the number of both long and short positions in a portfolio is important. We are most comfortable with long–short equity managers that take a concentrated approach to their long positions and a diversified approach to their short positions. So, to the extent that our hedge fund managers detail their activity over the course of the most recent quarter, we have a sound understanding of the execution of their strategies and, therefore, can apply attribution analysis to their performance analysis—analysis that we find extremely helpful.

At Ashbridge, about 25 percent of our clients' assets is invested in hedged strategies, of which about 40 percent is in trading and arbitrage strategies and 60 percent is in long–short equity. From a tax-efficiency standpoint, most of the fixed-income surrogate strategies will be taxed as short-term gains at approximately a 40 percent rate. Some long–short equity managers, however, depending on their mandate and approach, are able to recognize long-term gains for their clients, which are taxed at a more favorable 20 percent rate. Because so many of these managers invest in their own funds, it is also in their best interest to defer the gain to the extent that the deferral is a good investment decision. In general, hedged strategies may not be tax efficient, but the tax efficiency of funds varies on a case-by-case basis. We thus believe the opportunity exists for tax efficiency in long–short equity funds.

Catalysts for Changing a Manager

Several catalysts can lead us to change a manager we have selected. Once we recognize the presence of one of the catalysts, we monitor the manager until we are able to determine whether the situation is temporary or the beginning of a trend. Sustained underperformance relative to the benchmark and to peers over a three- or four-quarter period, inexplicable style drift, departure of key personnel from the organization, acquisition of the investment management firm, and change in the temperament of the portfolio manager—all are possible catalysts for recommending that a manager be dropped.

Catalysts Leading to Change. Inexplicable style drift is a concern because, in all likelihood, a manager is only one of at least six managers of a client's portfolio. Any change in style can wreak havoc on the client's asset allocation policy because a manager's initial mandate is designed to complement the styles and strategies of other managers. Style drift can significantly alter the overall risk–return profile of the client's portfolio, so we need to figure out why the drift is happening.

We also need to understand the implications of personnel changes in a manager's organization. Frequent changes in personnel are no longer unusual, but the impact of such changes on performance can be dramatic. The depth of the team managing the portfolio at the firm—multiple portfolio managers and analysts—can alleviate any problems arising from personnel turnover if the other team members can fill the role of the team member who left the firm. But in a smaller organization (for example, a firm with only five individuals), if the top one or two portfolio managers leave the firm, such a change will likely be a significant problem for the predictability of returns.

On a positive note, consolidation within the financial services industry has become so common that if a manager is acquired, the acquisition does not necessarily have negative consequences. Seven years ago, investors had to question the incentive of the manager when an acquisition occurred. Did the manager want to continue managing money? Were the proper incentives in place for him or her to continue managing aggressively and appropriately for the next three to five years after the acquisition? In the past three years, four or five of our managers have been acquired, but in only two cases did we make a managerial change 6–12 months after the acquisition.

A change in the temperament of a portfolio manager (a phenomenon our research director has deemed "the Ferrari syndrome") also causes us to sit up and take notice. A change in temperament alone is not a concern, but a manager's change in focus is, whether it is a greater desire to acquire "toys" or another type of diversion. It is a delicate issue, but sometimes the questions "How many houses or cars does the manager have?" or "What is happening in the manager's personal life?" must be addressed. Unless a manager's focus is purely on his or her fund, performance results will deviate from expectations.

Our experience has shown that a number of the catalysts that we have identified and that we monitor are bearers of bad tidings in terms of returns. During one of our regular conference calls in the spring of 1999 to a mid-cap growth manager, for instance, we discovered the portfolio manager had changed. The new portfolio manager did not understand the fund's mandate and was taking a barbell approach in his capitalization structure of the portfolio. His strategy was to buy small-cap and large-cap stocks to achieve a mean mid-cap weighting, which was not an appropriate approach within the context of the client's overall portfolio strategy. Our discovery resulted in an immediate transition to a new manager.

Another transition, which took a little longer to play out, occurred after one of our international value managers was acquired by a large firm with a growth orientation. Our understanding after the acquisition was that the manager we had hired would maintain his value bias, but in the course of our quarterly conference calls with the manager, we noticed the returns starting to falter. The stocks being purchased resembled growth stocks, and the value stocks were being sold. We knew from a risk standpoint in the client's overall portfolio that the loss of the value orientation was not acceptable. This change in manager style also coincided with a general shift away from growth and into value outperformance, and that general market shift was equally a problem. This variation from the initial mandate was the signal for us to change managers.

Another catalyst that spurred us to make a manager change had to do with a problem we had with one of our managed futures managers. We use managed futures strategies as an asset class that is truly uncorrelated with fixed-income and equity markets. As with hedged strategies, monitoring these managers, particularly the discretionary traders, is difficult, even though managed futures may have more transparency than hedged strategies. The manager we fired was a discretionary trader. His bets on the directions of various commodities and markets were becoming larger, and he was becoming more leveraged. Not surprisingly, the more positions started going against him, the more he started adding to them. Our response was to terminate our relationship with the manager.

Catalysts Not Leading to Change. For all of the catalysts that prove to be correct in indicating that a change in manager is necessary, just as many never lead to that conclusion. In the case of a large-cap growth manager we have used for an excess of 15 years and a mid-cap value manager we have used for about 5 years, we monitored periods of underperformance that could be rationalized by the managers. Wonderful performance had been achieved prior to this window of underperformance, and during the periods of underperformance, the managers maintained style consistency.

In the case of the growth manager, the manager simply could not justify the high multiples prevalent in 1998 and 1999, and his fund performed poorly relative to its benchmark, the Russell 1000 Growth Index, and its peer groups. Not surprisingly, this manager came into the 2000–2001 window with far less exposure to technology and a far more defensive portfolio, ready to weather the challenges of the past two years. Consequently, this manager has done a fabulous job at capital preservation for our clients, and although convincing clients of the strong points of this manager in 1999 was tough, clients are thrilled now.

Likewise, in the case of the mid-cap value manager, when value managers were tempted in 1999 to find ways to justify buying companies such as America Online and Microsoft Corporation and the more moderately priced technology stocks with lower multiples, this manager simply would not do so. This manager was targeting the cheapest quintile of stocks within his universe, the Russell 1000 Index, when these stocks were dramatically underperforming other market sectors. The manager stuck by his value orientation, and his performance for the 18 months beginning April 2000 has been phenomenal.

Although clients are not always comfortable with the volatility of some of their managers' performance, if a good reason exists to stay the course with a manager through bad times, clients can be substantially rewarded. And from a tax standpoint, remaining with this large-cap growth manager and mid-cap value manager was very much in these clients' best interests.

Transferring a Taxable Portfolio to a New Manager

How do we handle a transition from one manager to another, particularly in the context of working with a new client? A client rarely walks in the door with uninvested cash. Clients usually have a variety of investments they have bought along the way or have a concentrated holding they may or may not have already begun to diversify. In some cases, a client may already be working with a consultant and may have a variety of managers that are too highly correlated or are underperforming. We typically propose an asset allocation that includes the managers we would recommend and try to match the client's current portfolio as closely as we can with some combination of our recommended managers.

When we initially qualify a manager, we want to know that a high degree of the manager's clients are taxable clients and that the manager has acquired a comfort and experience level in working with the taxable investor. We want to be familiar with the tax-savings techniques the manager uses, such as tax-loss harvesting, swapping into similar stocks, or using ETFs to maintain exposure to a sector to avoid the 31-day wash-sale rule. We also seek assurance that the manager has transitioned portfolios in the past into the manager's model portfolio and want to know approximately how long the transition period will be. Ideally, we prefer a two- to three-year period. If the transition drags on any longer, performance will deviate from expectations for too long and the client will become dissatisfied. The family hired the manager with a specific mandate, yet the manager could be handicapped by the portfolio that he or she has to transition, so a balance has to be struck between getting through the transition process quickly and being prudent.

We also want to monitor the performance of that manager during the transition process, even though we understand that the manager's performance may deviate from the performance of his or her typical model portfolio. Consequently, we may adopt strict performance standards during the migration period to account for divergences in portfolio structure and attribution. Thus, one way of transitioning to a new manager is to start with an existing portfolio, find a manager or managers similar to the existing managers, and allow the new manager to move through the transition steps over a period of time. This type of transition can be done fairly reasonably.

Another transition approach we have used for a client or prospective client with only six or seven managers is to evaluate the portfolio from a tax standpoint to determine where, in a tax-efficient manner, we can raise cash. We then identify losses available to offset gains, sell the selected securities, and invest the proceeds generated with the new managers. Giving managers cash is easy, but analyzing the overall portfolio holdings from a tax perspective is complicated. The process becomes even trickier when the portfolio has a significant embedded gain. Prudence often dictates spacing out the sale of the appreciated securities over a certain period of time and incurring the capital gains tax liability on the sales in different tax years, preferably selling early in the tax year and deferring the tax liability for another 15 months (e.g., sale in January and tax payment in April of the following year). As the appreciated stock is sold, the manager has the opportunity to complement the remaining as-yet-unsold appreciated stock with new stock purchases and also to distinguish and highlight the style he or she has been employed to manage. At the same time, we want that manager to carefully monitor the holdings that are retained. In light of the accounting scandals at Enron Corporation, Global Crossing, and Tyco International, monitoring holdings is as important as monitoring managers, if not more so. And regardless of the tax consequences, if a manager perceives problems in a company, we are inclined to sell the holding. Investment decisions should outweigh pure tax considerations, and we encourage feedback from managers about such issues.

Conclusion

Initially selecting a manager is a challenging task, but the hard work pays off in finding superior managers. Equally challenging is the ongoing monitoring of these managers, and perhaps not surprisingly, we use the same quantitative and qualitative criteria to both select and monitor managers. Monitoring managers, however, does require some unique evaluation criteria, and monitoring hedge fund managers in particular, with their lack of transparency, leverage, and high betas, further complicates the process.

Even with careful initial selection of a manager, the monitoring process sometimes reveals changes in a manager's process or firm that require us to terminate the manager in order to maintain the targets that have been set for our clients. But these manager deviations, or catalysts for change, have to be evaluated carefully. Although these catalysts have prompted us to change a manager, they do not always do so. If the deviations occur for a good reason, we will stand by the manager and explain the situation to our clients.

If we are to be good consultants, we must see our roles as questioners, skeptics, and also advocates for managers. At Ashbridge, we value a rigorous approach to our initial due diligence and ongoing monitoring of managers and believe that our efforts will create and sustain the best managerial performance at the most reasonable level of risk for our clients. We feel strongly that asking good questions and constantly seeking better answers are vital aspects of our manager-selection process.

Question and Answer Session

Louisa W. Sellers

Question: Do you recommend passive or active management?

Sellers: In some asset classes, managers can add alpha, and in others, particularly those with underlying indexes that have inherently less turnover, active managers may add less value. A large-cap index fund can play a role in a portfolio and can be complemented by specialist managers in the asset classes that have been proven to be less efficient.

During the past couple of years, so much turnover has occurred within the Russell 2000 Index—with about 500–600 different stocks entering and exiting the index—that the Russell 2000 is probably not a tax-efficient proxy for the small-cap market. Therefore, an active manager for this asset class makes sense. Likewise, although I can't quantify the number of stocks that roll in and out of the MSCI Europe/Australasia/Far East (EAFE) Index on an annual basis, I suspect that number is relatively high. In contrast, only 20–30 names change in the S&P 500 on an annual basis. Because the S&P 500 doesn't have a lot of turnover in its composition each year, it can be a reasonable proxy for the large-cap market; thus, the large-cap market is an asset class that does not typically require active management.

Question: How do you justify your role as an intermediary in terms of the value added to the overall return in your clients' portfolios?

Sellers: Typically, a family turns to a consultant if the amount of assets the family has to give to any single manager is not that great. So, if the consultant can aggregate those assets with those of other investors, the consultant can negotiate lower amounts to invest with a manager for an individual family. Usually, we can also garner lower fees because the manager doesn't have to talk with each of our clients on an ongoing basis—only with us, four times a year.

We add value because we can reduce the manager's fee and help the client achieve superior returns. Our reporting process shows how each manager is performing against his or her appropriate benchmark index, and then we create a blended index for the overall portfolio in which we show the magnitude of manager outperformance over that benchmark of underlying indexes. We can make a compelling case that our managers are adding significant alpha over time. Even in equity markets that have had a relatively flat return for the past three years, our portfolios have been compounding at a rate of 8–10 percent a year. Most of our clients are satisfied with the work we've done because we have created a positively compounding return despite the volatile market.

Question: How much do you emphasize tax efficiency in your manager-selection process?

Sellers: In the long-only strategies, we can select from hundreds of managers, so it boils down to a judgment call. Once we narrow the group to the 20 percent we are interested in, a myriad of factors narrows the group even further. Perhaps the manager is geared more toward institutional investors, or perhaps the manager's fees or minimum account size limit are high. In our dialogue with a manager, if we hear that the manager has high turnover with little consideration of harvesting losses to offset realized gains, we know that this inattention to tax efficiency is not ideal for our clients.

At the same time, if tax efficiency were the only criterion we cared about, we would lose many wonderful managers we've worked with over time that in some years have demonstrated high tax efficiency and in others have taken substantial gains because they felt that was the right thing to do from an investment standpoint.

Question: How truthful are investment management firms about the departure of key individuals? Do you ever confirm the firm's stated reason for the individual's departure with the individual who left the firm?

Sellers: So far, the information we have been given has been truthful. We try to find out where people go after they leave and the reason they left because they can provide key information. This information can tell us a lot about the firm we are presumably staying with, and sometimes, we uncover issues that make us uncomfortable.

Question: What do you look for in your initial due diligence and quarterly interviews with managers?

Sellers: Selecting and then staying with a manager comes down to two key factors—competence and chemistry. In the face-to-face interviews, we hope to determine the synergy between the managers, traders, and analysts. If they have a great deal of enthusiasm and a passion for what they're doing, they will probably do a good job. If an aura of negativity surrounds a manager, it will ultimately spill over into the results achieved in the portfolio.

This aspect of the manager-selection process is more art than science; it cannot be quantified. What comes out of the face-to-face meetings is simply what we observe and how we are treated by the team we are talking to. If the manager has an interest in Ashbridge's client base, what we do, and how we want to work with the manager, that positive attitude will go a long way with us. If we happen to catch someone on a bad day, we're willing to give him or her the benefit of the doubt and come back again, but the confidence we have in a manager is derived from our initial impressions during these interviews.

Question: What does an investment management firm that has been acquired or is no longer independent have to do to avoid getting fired?

Sellers: One of the best examples of this situation is a firm we had worked with for about six years before it was acquired. Right after the announcement was made and the disclosure became public, we received a call from the lead portfolio manager about what had happened so that we would know about it before finding the story in the press.

From our quarterly interviews, we learned the portfolio manager hated the tedium of the paperwork of the takeover. He was clearly annoyed about the takeover getting in the way of his research and his passion for stock picking. He was probably thrilled about the compensation he would receive from the acquisition, but he clearly wanted to be able to focus on managing the portfolio, which was a great sign.

Even better was the fact that when we had an involved conversation with him before our regularly scheduled call, we learned that an abundance of research had been done on a sector of stocks that the manager wanted to add to the portfolio. Sure enough, when the market gave him a buying opportunity, his firm took advantage of it. So, even while this deal was being negotiated, intensive and relevant research was still being done.

Question: With regard to hedge fund manager information, does your firm place any weight on the monetary commitment in the fund from the manager of the fund in terms of the manager's participation?

Sellers: We always prefer to work with managers whose free assets are tied up in the firm and the fund. Such a situation aligns the manager's interests with the interests of our clients.

Question: Significant outperformance by hedge funds seems to be concentrated in the earliest years of a fund's existence. How does this early outperformance influence your decisions?

Sellers: When a portfolio is small, it is easier for managers to execute their ideas. As a fund grows, however, challenges arise. Having said that, we like to see a long track record. We want to see monthly results, and we want to see consistency in those results and the market conditions under which they were achieved.

Rather than act quickly and risk ending up with a poor result, we prefer to miss 6 or 12 months of good performance in order to assure ourselves that this fund is a place that our clients will be happy for a long time, especially when we are hiring a hedge fund manager. And because of the lockup periods of hedge funds, we have to be especially confident in a manager because our clients will be invested with that manager for at least 12 months and possibly longer. So, hedge funds are no place to be second-guessing those initial decisions.

Question: Is there a particular hedge fund strategy that you would recommend for high-net-worth clients?

Sellers: We think there is much greater opportunity for private clients, for high-net-worth families, to understand a long–short equity strategy than market-neutral pairs trading, for example. Private clients are quite accepting of the idea that there are qualified managers in the industry who can identify companies expected to appreciate in value. And as part of that same process, private clients realize these managers have the ability to identify other companies with deteriorating fundamentals or poor management structures—whatever that catalyst may be—that will drive the stock price down and enable the manager to short the stock profitably.

An important part of our role as an intermediary is educating clients so that they feel comfortable with the strategies we recommend. There is something satisfying about recommending an investment approach to a client that can reduce the client's portfolio risk and have it be one the client can understand.

123
Improving Tax Efficiency with Derivatives

Jean L.P. Brunel, CFA
Managing Principal
Brunel Associates, LLC
Edina, Minnesota

> Important tax-law caveats and potential risks notwithstanding, certain derivatives strategies can significantly improve after-tax portfolio returns by altering the timing of the execution decision and hence the need to pay capital gains taxes. Derivatives also give managers the flexibility to separate their decisions in terms of strategic asset allocation, portfolio rebalancing, and security selection from the implementation of these decisions. These hybrid physical/derivatives solutions can greatly reduce tax costs, but they cannot be used by all investors.

Using derivatives to improve tax efficiency is a fascinating, if challenging, topic. Unfortunately, the complexity of many of the strategies I will be talking about in this presentation makes them, for the time being at least, the province of the ultra wealthy, not those with investable assets of only $1 million. Nevertheless, the topic is interesting because it illustrates an essential element of the understanding of tax efficiency: Tax efficiency requires the advisor to challenge conventional wisdom and think outside the box. Most of us who are advisors to private clients started our careers in the institutional world before switching to the private client world. And although we have learned a lot, most of what we have learned, unfortunately, is not applicable to the world of individual investors.

In this presentation, I will discuss the reasons why tax efficiency through the use of derivatives will inevitably grow as the industry becomes more sophisticated in the way it serves the private wealth management market. In particular, derivatives can enhance tax efficiency because they allow advisors to change the timing of the execution of the investment decision. Thus, I will talk about the importance of timing and illustrate a few strategies that allow advisors to alter the timing of the execution. Derivatives also allow advisors to segregate the decisions that they make along three dimensions (strategic asset allocation, periodic portfolio rebalancing, and security selection) and to vary the execution of these decisions according to different investing instruments. The prime caveat is, however, that derivatives raise a number of risks that do not exist in the physical securities world.

Timing of the Execution Decision

A taxable investor needs to focus on all the costs associated with an execution decision and thus on the timing of the key decision points. Before discussing the importance of the timing of the execution decision, however, I want to take a couple of steps back and dissect a transaction.

Transaction Costs. Institutional investors have been blessed by changes in the industry that are allowing them to almost forget about transaction costs, and yet, for taxable investors, these transaction costs remain important because taxes are one of the components of these costs.

In general, every investor, taxable or tax exempt, should be concerned about brokerage costs and the market impact of execution. But investors have been the beneficiaries of substantially decreasing brokerage commissions during the past 20 years, and now, a large number of investors are able to trade at commissions of between 1 and 5 cents a share. Therefore, many portfolio managers tend to almost ignore brokerage costs, which, indeed, are now only a small fraction of the total transaction costs. Market impact used to be a significant consideration, but the creation of electronic communication networks and the greater focus on dedicated trading functions have reduced bid–ask spreads and, hence, the market impact of a particular trade. Although those costs are not zero, they are not absolutely critical to the decision-making process.

But brokerage costs and market impact is where the average institutional investor or tax-exempt investor stops worrying. Everything beyond that point does not exist for them. They do not have to worry about whether they will have to pay capital gains taxes if they sell a particular security or about the composition (income versus capital gains) of returns. If they decide to switch out of a straight equity investment into convertible securities, which might be particularly cheap at that moment, they are changing the composition of their anticipated return from a predominately capital return to a predominately income return. The consequences of that change are that the costs, taxwise, will be different.

That the individual investor needs to think about these other costs introduces what I call the "curse of the taxable investor": More often than not, the individual investor pays twice for any mistake. The first cost associated with a bad investment decision is generating negative alpha. The second cost associated with a bad investment decision is paying capital gains taxes on that negative alpha. Note that I said negative alpha, not negative returns. Therein lies an important point. A transaction that produces negative alpha still likely requires the investor to pay for the privilege of having made a poor investment decision. Regardless of the fact that the alpha was negative, if the investor made money from the investment, Uncle Sam wants his share. Sir John Templeton said that, on average, he never met anyone who was right more than 65 percent of the time. The corollary to that statement has to be that investors are wrong at least 35 percent of the time, so individual investors pay taxes at least 35 percent of the time for the privilege of making a bad decision.

For a tax-conscious investor, all trades must be viewed from both the buy side and the sell side. To buy an instrument deemed attractive, the investor must raise the funds through the sale of another security; to sell an instrument deemed unattractive, the investor must reinvest the funds by purchasing another security. The attractiveness of the security the investor wants to buy is a direct function of the cost associated with the security the investor is going to sell. Imagine the case, which is not uncommon these days, of an investor who owns only one stock worth $100 with a basis of zero. That investor will find it difficult, based on comparative investment return expectations alone, to transact. Making such a switch means that the investor has to jump a high hurdle in that the costs associated with selling the low-basis stock must be exceeded by the returns expected on the smaller total dollars invested in the new security. (The dollars fall because the proceeds from the sale are reduced by the payment of the tax liability associated with the capital gain.)

As an aside, notice that this cost implication makes the practice of recommending stocks for individual investors completely illogical when the recommender does not have knowledge of the details of the investor's portfolio. What may make sense for one investor's portfolio may not make sense for another investor's portfolio. The recommendation could be a complete catastrophe because the stock the investor would have to sell to buy the recommended stock might trigger a substantial gain for the investor, thus requiring the investor to pay sizable capital gains taxes. These taxes could raise the bar so high for the switch that the returns expected from the recommended security could not reasonably be expected to exceed the returns associated with continuing to hold the low-basis security.

Physical Transaction. Most investors do not fully appreciate the transaction sequence when dealing with physical securities. The process starts when the investor has an investment idea and then executes it. When the investor executes the idea, more often than not (assuming that capital market returns are positive in the long term) the investor will have to pay some form of capital gains tax on the sale of the security, whose proceeds the investor expects to reinvest in the new security. Notice that the investor pays the tax on the security sold before knowing whether the transaction produces a favorable result. Again, sometimes (about 35 percent of the time according to Sir John Templeton) the investor pays taxes for the privilege of making a poor decision.

Derivatives Transaction. By using derivative instruments, the investor can change the sequence of the transaction steps. That is, by using derivatives, the sequence starts with the investor's idea and then the execution of that idea (as with the physical transaction), but the investor is able to observe the results of the transaction before paying any capital gains taxes (the reverse of the physical transaction situation). This situation reflects the fact that, technically, a derivative security purchase is an "opening trade" and thus usually does not constitute a taxable event. Taxes, if any, will be due when the trade is "closed," at which point the investor will know whether the trade was profitable or not.

Changing the Timing: Security-Selection Driven. In this section, I provide four examples of how derivatives can be used to change the timing of the execution at the security-selection level: collars, variable prepaid forwards (VPFs), hedged double-up transactions, and intentional wash-sale triggers. The first two strategies (collars and VPFs) are useful for diversifying low-basis stock positions. The second two strategies (hedged double-up and intentional wash-sale triggers) are useful option strategies that lower the risk of holding a stock.[1]

■ *Collars.* To create a collar on a low-basis stock (or on any stock), the investor first buys a put. By buying this put, the investor creates a floor under the price of the security and ensures that the stock will not experience a substantial loss from the price at which it was bought. At the same time, the investor finances the put by writing a call at a higher strike price. The difference between the strike price of the put and the strike price of the call determines the nature of the collar. If the premium on the call is higher than the premium on the put, the investor will have created an income-producing collar. If the premiums on the two options are equal, the investor will have created a cashless collar. In some instances the investor might want to retain the rights to a substantial amount of appreciation, in which case the premium the investor receives from writing the call will be less than the premium paid for purchasing the put. Importantly, when a low-basis stock is collared, the investor has increased both the ability to monetize the position by borrowing against it and the opportunity to borrow against it more cost-effectively; the investor now has a position that is considerably less risky because it can be viewed as collateral by a potential lender.

■ *Variable prepaid forwards.* With VPFs, the investor enters into a contract to sell stock at some future date. The investor receives a cash advance up front, usually 70–80 percent of the notional value of the contract. The amount of the advance is driven in large measure by the implied interest rate, which means that the term of the contract also effectively drives the amount of the advance. What makes a VPF transaction attractive on an after-tax basis is that the amount of stock the investor delivers varies according to the price of the stock at some future point in time. For instance, suppose you and I agree today that I will deliver to you in three years 1,000 shares of XYZ Company at $60 a share. In three years, then, I will deliver $60,000 worth of stock to you. If XYZ stock rises modestly until at the end of the three-year period XYZ is $70 a share, under most contract structures, instead of delivering 1,000 shares, I would deliver the number of shares that would equal $60,000.

---
[1] For more information on collars and VPFs, see Scott D. Welch, "Diversifying Concentrated Holdings," and Robert N. Gordon, "Hedging Low-Cost-Basis Stock," *Investment Counseling for Private Clients III* (Charlottesville, VA: AIMR, 2001), pp. 30–35, 36–44.

Under this complex structure, a VPF resembles an unbalanced collar. An unbalanced collar, in my definition, is simply a collar for which the investor has sold fewer calls than the number of puts he or she has bought. In both instances (the collar and the VPF), note that the investor will be selling stock at some future point in time rather than today, which means that the investor has the opportunity to earn a return on money that otherwise would be paid to the government in the form of capital gains taxes.

The investor does not have to own low-basis stock for these two strategies to work. For instance, suppose an investor holds an appreciated stock (but not necessarily with a low basis) in his or her portfolio. In some cases, buying a put might make more sense than selling the stock. For example, if the investor's view of the stock in the long term is favorable but the investor is worried that over an interim period the stock might be exposed to price pressures, then buying a put may be preferable to selling the stock outright. This strategy would have been a good one to use a couple of years ago when high-tech stocks appeared to have value in the long term but seemed overvalued in the short term.

■ *Hedged double up.* The hedged double-up strategy and the intentional wash-sale triggers are more complicated than collars and VPFs. I do not recommend these strategies for all investors, but including them in this presentation is important because they illustrate the need for thinking outside the box. Both strategies involve a situation in which the investor has a loss in a security. The investor would like to realize that loss in order to offset a capital gain but has a favorable long-term view on the stock and does not want to sell it.

The technique that has been used for years in this type of situation is called "doubling up." If the investor has a loss, the investor doubles up on the stock (doubles the size of the position), and in 31 days, the investor sells one of the two sets of stock, the one with the largest capital loss. This technique makes no sense. How many investors maintain a cash balance in their portfolios so that when they want to double up, they happen to have money available to do so? In fact, most of the doubling up historically has involved selling something, probably at a gain, so that the investor can buy a stock on which the investor has a loss. The other problem is that in a number of instances, doubling up can look like throwing good money after bad.

Doubling up can be done in a way that lets the investor avoid getting caught in the tax net. This technique, hedged double up, involves borrowing to buy the second position on the stock in question. Suppose I have a stock, LMN, in which I have a loss.

I want to take the loss but cannot because I also want to own the stock. I decide to borrow to buy LMN. This borrowing may seem irrational because I appear to be leveraging the portfolio, and it would perhaps be irrational if I stopped there. But my next step, after buying the second parcel of the stock, is to buy a put and sell a call at the same strike price. By buying a put and selling a call, I will effectively earn the risk-free rate, and I have eliminated any potential damage to my portfolio from the future movement in the price of the stock I bought (my double-up position). I have created synthetic cash, provided I am dealing in large enough quantities that I do not get slaughtered on the volatility spread built into the option valuation. The cost for this transaction is, more or less, my own credit premium because it will be the cost of my loan, which is equal to the risk-free interest rate plus the profit of the bank and reflects in part the bank's funding cost but in part my creditworthiness minus the risk-free rate.

Intentional wash-sale trigger. The key to the intentional wash-sale trigger is that an investor can trigger the wash-sale rule only once. Suppose I own LMN and have a loss in LMN I would like to take, but I like LMN in the long term and would like to maintain exposure to it. What do I do? I could sell my LMN stock and buy a call on LMN. If I buy a call option on a security that I just sold to take a loss, then I will trigger the wash-sale rule. In triggering the wash-sale rule, that loss will not be immediately recognized; the loss must be incorporated into the basis of the security I have just bought. So, my loss in LMN has been transferred to my basis in the call option. But having triggered the wash-sale rule once, I cannot trigger it again. I, therefore, buy back my LMN stock.

If I stopped at this point, I would own both the stock and the call option, which involves some—potentially significant—increase in specific risk. Furthermore, I would not have realized the loss in the stock (now effectively transferred to the call option), which was the reason for doing the trade in the first place. So, in theory, a one-day delay in the transaction (I own the stock and the option for a day) allows me to adhere to the letter of the law, although holding the position for a few more days might be safer.

Changing the Timing: Asset Allocation Driven. Derivatives can also be used to change the timing of the taxable execution of investment decisions at the asset allocation level. Imagine that an investor had a perfectly balanced portfolio of international stocks at the beginning of the year, but by mid-March, the Japanese equity market rose 13 percent and the French equity market decreased 0.5 percent. If the portfolio was well balanced on January 1, it cannot possibly be well balanced in mid-March because of the fluctuations in the values of the stocks in the portfolio.

One option is for the investor to rebalance the portfolio through the sale and purchase of individual securities. The investor can buy French stocks and sell Japanese stocks, but this situation harkens back to the curse of the individual investor. Another way to handle the problem is to sell Japanese equity futures and buy French equity futures. In doing so, the investor has opened transactions rather than closed transactions; therefore, the investor is not liable for taxes until the transaction is closed at some future point in time. In this way, the investor has been able to rebalance the portfolio and prevent it from drifting without incurring a tax associated with a capital gain.

That strategy can be taken a step further. Investors can use the same transaction to execute a view they would like to pursue instead of using the transaction to maintain a portfolio's balance. If an investor likes French stocks, that investor can buy French stocks and sell U.K. stocks through the futures markets without upsetting the underlying physical positions of his or her portfolio. Thus, derivatives can be used to tactically alter country or market-cap allocations. For instance, an investor can go short S&P 500 Index contracts and go long S&P 600 Index contracts if the investor wants greater exposure to small stocks. A similar strategy can be used for the style indexes if the investor wants to be long growth and short value, or vice versa.

Ultimately, managers need to understand that using derivatives is an important strategy for altering the balance in a portfolio without triggering the curse of the taxable investor.

Segregating Decision Axis and Execution

Not only can derivatives be used to change the timing of the execution of investment decisions (or perhaps more precisely, the timing of incurring capital gains taxes), but they can also be used to segregate the decision axis from the execution of the transactions.

Returns in a portfolio come from three traditional sources. The first is strategic asset allocation. As nearly all managers know, a massive amount of ink and paper has been used to demonstrate that a large proportion of the returns of any portfolio is a function of its long-term asset allocation. Periodic portfolio rebalancing is the second source of return. This source covers a wide variety of strategies—from preventing portfolio drift to active asset allocation (in either the volatility capture or the comparative value sense) to market timing. The final source of return is security selection—buying and selling individual securities in order to outperform the market.

The important point is that all three of these axes normally require the manager to transact in individual securities.

Hybrid Solutions. What if the manager could segregate each of the decision axes and apply to each axis a particular execution mechanism that does not overlap with the execution mechanism for another axis? A hybrid approach to a multiasset class or multistrategy portfolio segregates decisions by instrument. With security selection, the manager does not have much of a choice; the manager has to transact in individual securities. But the manager can do strategic asset allocation through long-term swaps, and the manager can do portfolio rebalancing through index futures.

I will illustrate this point by showing an "experiment" that I published in the *Journal of Wealth Management* in 1999.[2] In this experiment, I wanted to keep things simple, so I used a global equity portfolio. This approach, however, can also (conceptually at least) be used for balanced portfolios. The target was to have 60 percent of the portfolio in large-cap U.S. stocks (S&P 500 Index), 15 percent in small-cap U.S. stocks (Russell 2000 Index), and 25 percent in non-U.S. equities (MSCI Europe/Australasia/Far East [EAFE] Index). This allocation can be achieved in several ways, but the manager has just four decision variables: security selection value added, tax efficiency of security selection, tactical asset allocation alpha, and periodic portfolio rebalancing.

■ *Security selection value added.* The first decision variable is security selection value added. The manager can use indexed portfolios, in which case the manager is basically saying that active managers cannot add value. Alternatively, the manager can seek active management alpha, which presupposes that the manager believes in active management.

■ *Tax efficiency of security selection.* The second variable is the tax efficiency of security selection. All managers know that they cannot expect a tax-efficient security selection process to produce pretax returns equivalent to the returns from a tax-oblivious process. It stands to reason that the more constraints imposed on the manager, the more likely that the manager will be unable to execute a transaction at the margin that under less constrained circumstances the manager would have been able to execute; the manager is thus leaving some alpha on the table.

■ *Tactical asset allocation alpha.* The third variable is tactical asset allocation alpha. The manager must decide whether active management can produce tactical asset allocation alpha. Do managers have the ability to market time domestic versus international equities or large-cap versus small-cap equities?

■ *Periodic portfolio rebalancing.* The final variable addresses the rebalancing of the portfolio. In this experiment, the portfolio has a static benchmark. So, if the portfolio holds more than one asset class or strategy, then the relative performance differential across these asset classes or strategies will lead them to drift toward overweighted or underweighted positions, depending on whether they have outperformed or underperformed the rest of the portfolio. The manager has the choice of either letting the portfolio drift or systematically rebalancing it.

Implementation Methods. The manager has eight possible approaches to rebalancing: five physical-only solutions and three hybrid physical/derivatives solutions.

In this experiment, I began by investing 100 percent of the portfolio in tax-efficient large-cap equities and ignoring margin requirements because they complicate matters. I chose large-cap equities because of the lack of an adequate small-cap tax-efficient process at the time. In the hybrid strategies (the last three proposed solutions), I created the systematic strategic exposure to non-U.S. large-cap equities (EAFE) of 25 percent and to small-cap U.S equities (Russell 2000) of 15 percent by using 5-year swaps. (If I were doing this experiment today, I would use 5.5-year contracts because the most recent tax change now provides for an 8 percent capital gains tax treatment if the contract runs five years and one day.) Then, once a year, I used index futures to rebalance the portfolio when I wanted to combat drift.

Clearly, straddle rules need to be considered. I am making the assumption that I could use approximate, but not exactly the same, indexes in executing the derivatives strategies. For instance, I am assuming that the Russell 1000 can be used instead of the S&P 500 as a proxy for large-cap U.S. equities in the swap transaction. This type of substitution creates basis risk but also allows the strategy to work within the boundaries of what the tax laws will allow.

■ *Physical-only solutions.* The first and simplest approach is to physically invest in the three strategies (large-cap U.S., small-cap U.S., and EAFE stocks) in an indexed manner and allow the portfolio to drift uncorrected. This approach is the ultimate form of a buy-and-hold strategy. The second approach is a partially active approach with drift. The large-cap

---
[2] Jean L.P. Brunel, "A Tax-Aware Approach to the Management of Multiasset Class Portfolios," *Journal of Wealth Management* (Spring 1999):57–70.

U.S. allocation is actively managed in a tax-aware manner; the other two strategies are indexed and are allowed to drift without being rebalanced. The third approach is the same as the second, except once a year, the portfolio is moved back to its strategic balance; drift is not allowed. The fourth approach is to actively manage all the asset classes, but only the large-cap U.S. allocation is managed in a tax-aware manner (i.e., the management of the other two classes is tax oblivious), and the portfolio is systematically rebalanced. The fifth all-physical approach is the same as the fourth except tactical asset allocation (TAA) is used to create additional alpha.

Hybrid physical/derivatives solutions. As I explained earlier, the hybrid global equity portfolio in my experiment consisted of one physical strategy (100 percent large-cap U.S. equities managed in a tax-aware manner), two derivatives overlays—a five-year swap into 15 percent small-cap U.S. equities (Russell 2000) and a five-year swap into 25 percent non-U.S. equities (large-cap EAFE)—and one annual rebalancing tool (index futures). The three hybrid physical/derivatives solutions are a hybrid mix with drift, a hybrid mix systematically rebalanced, and a hybrid mix with annual TAA rebalancing.

Table 1 tracks the impact of the various sources of value added from the physical-only solutions as the portfolio moves from a fully indexed mix with drift to a portfolio of actively managed physical security exposures to a hybrid portfolio with all three asset classes with TAA insights. Notice for the All Active with TAA Portfolio, the predicted and observed pretax returns were the same, 10.64 percent. For the hybrid solutions, shown in **Table 2**, notice that the predicted and observed pretax returns for the Non-Large-Cap Swapped with TAA Portfolio were identical, 10.54 percent. Therefore, compared with the physical-only solution, the hybrid solution produced negative value added on a pretax basis (–10 bps), which should not be surprising because these portfolios are paying for a strategy that can be executed at a much lower cost by buying index funds.

The important question is what happens on an after-tax basis? Remember that I said at the beginning of this presentation that individual investors pay for the privilege of making bad decisions because of the tax implications. **Table 3** shows the after-tax results—the tax implications—for the physical solutions. I must disclose that Table 3 exaggerates the impact of taxes because I have applied the tax liability at the level of the subportfolio, which is not truly a tax-aware approach. The truly tax-aware approach is to apply the tax liability at the level of the overall portfolio. By definition, I am thus exaggerating the tax impact on the active, tax-oblivious equity sub-

Table 1. Physical-Only Solutions: Pretax Returns

Measure	Predicted	Observed
Fully Indexed Drift Portfolio	7.965%	7.965%
Tax-aware large-cap alpha	1.360	1.366
Non-Large-Cap Indexed Drift Portfolio	9.325	9.330
Systematic rebalancing impact	–0.020	–0.020
Non-Large-Cap Indexed Rebalanced Portfolio	9.305	9.310
Non-tax-aware value added	0.809	0.807
Small-cap stocks	0.302	
EAFE stocks	0.507	
All Active No TAA Portfolio	10.114	10.117
TAA alpha	0.524	0.520
All Active with TAA Portfolio	10.637	10.637

Note: Tax-aware large-cap pretax alpha is equal to 1.360% (2.27% × 60%); non-tax-aware non-large-cap value added is equal to 0.809% [(2.01% × 15%) + (2.03% × 25%)].

Table 2. Hybrid Solutions: Pretax Returns

Measure	Predicted	Observed
Non-Large-Cap Indexed Drift Portfolio	9.325%	9.330%
Tax-aware value added on non-large-cap exposure	0.907	0.910
Swap costs:		
Small-cap stocks	0.105	
EAFE stocks	0.138	
Non-Large-Cap Swapped Drift Portfolio	9.989	9.998
Systematic rebalancing impact	0.027	0.027
Non-Large-Cap Swapped Rebalanced Portfolio	10.016	10.025
TAA alpha	0.524	0.515
Non-Large-Cap Swapped with TAA Portfolio	10.540	10.540

Note: Tax-aware large-cap pretax alpha is equal to 1.360% (2.27% × 60%); non-tax-aware non-large-cap value added is equal to 0.809% [(2.01% × 15%) + (2.03% × 25%)].

portfolios. The important point is that the observed tax efficiency of the 40 percent (25 percent EAFE and 15 percent Russell 2000) of my portfolio that is invested in tax-oblivious security selection is only 5.7 percent. In other words, I went into the process assuming the tax efficiency would be 73 percent. The difference between those two tax efficiency numbers (73 percent predicted and 5.7 percent observed) is the cost of making a bad decision. Even worse are the TAA alpha numbers. Note that I calibrated the model estimating that I could generate roughly 42 bps of after-tax TAA alpha. The observed after-tax TAA alpha was only 1.8 bps. Thus, the bulk of my TAA

Table 3. Physical Solutions: After Tax

Measure	Returns Predicted	Returns Observed	Tax Efficiency Predicted	Tax Efficiency Observed
Fully Indexed Drift Portfolio	7.766%	7.710%	97.5%	96.8%
Tax-aware large-cap alpha	1.319	1.304	97.0	95.5
Non-Large-Cap Indexed Drift Portfolio	9.085	9.014		96.6
Systematic rebalancing impact	–0.11	–0.109		
Non-Large-Cap Indexed Rebalanced Portfolio	8.976	8.904		95.6
Non-tax-aware value added	0.590	0.046		5.7
Small-cap stocks	0.220		73.0	
EAFE stocks	0.370		73.0	
All Active No TAA Portfolio	9.566	8.950		88.5
TAA alpha	0.419	0.018	80.0	3.4
All Active with TAA Portfolio	9.985	8.968		84.3

Note: Tax-aware value added on non-large-cap exposure is equal to 0.907% (2.27% × 40%).

---

alpha was lost because of the tax circumstances (i.e., the capital gains tax liability that resulted from the periodic rebalancing).

The next step is to look at the after-tax efficiency of the hybrid derivatives strategies, as shown in **Table 4**. The hybrid solutions, as compared with the physical solutions, had a 9 bp value-added shortfall on a pretax basis, but after tax, the hybrid solutions show a 102 bp positive contribution (9.987 percent hybrid observed minus 8.968 percent physical observed). Swap costs were quoted to me by a third party when I originally set up the experiment. I have not, however, accounted for the increase in risk associated with the basis risk taken in the experiment.

An important point to appreciate is that tax efficiency does not mean that the investor avoids taxes, only that the investor defers unavoidable taxes. Thus, tax-efficient management involves postponing the day of reckoning. Therefore, managing in a tax-aware manner causes the spread between the market value of the portfolio and the book value of the portfolio to widen over time. Eventually, in a liquidation scenario when securities are sold, a tax-efficient portfolio will incur a higher liquidation penalty than a tax-oblivious portfolio because the spread between market value and book value will be greater than if the portfolio were managed in a tax-oblivious manner. **Table 5** shows that the pre-liquidation benefit

Table 4. Hybrid Solutions: After Tax

Measure	Returns Predicted	Returns Observed	Tax Efficiency Predicted	Tax Efficiency Observed
Non-Large-Cap Indexed Drift Portfolio	9.085%	9.014%	97.5%	96.6%
Tax-aware value added on non-large-cap exposure	0.787	0.846	97.0	92.9
Swap costs:				
Small-cap stocks	0.105		100.0	
EAFE stocks	0.138		100.0	
Non-Large-Cap Swapped Drift Portfolio	9.629	9.617		96.2
Systematic rebalancing impact	0.017	0.017		
Non-Large-Cap Swapped Rebalanced Portfolio	9.646	9.634		96.1
TAA alpha	0.419	0.353	80.0	68.6
Non-Large-Cap Swapped with TAA Portfolio	10.065	9.987		94.8

Note: Tax-aware value added on non-large-cap exposure is 0.91% [97% (2.27% × 40%)].

Table 5. Post-Liquidation Penalties

Measure	Tax-Efficiency Pre-Liquidation	Tax-Efficiency Post-Liquidation	Post-Liquidation Penalty
All Indexed, Drift	96.8%	84.4%	12.8%
Non-Large-Cap Indexed, Drift	96.6	84.8	12.3
Non-Large-Cap Indexed, Rebalanced	95.6	84.6	11.5
All Active No TAA	88.5	81.8	7.5
All Active with TAA	84.3	78.4	7.0
Non-Large-Cap Swapped Drift	96.2	84.8	11.8
Non-Large-Cap Swapped Rebalanced	96.1	84.8	11.7
Non-Large-Cap Swapped with TAA	94.8	84.0	11.3

between All Active with TAA and the Non-Large-Cap Swapped with TAA (the hybrid solution) shrinks post liquidation. On a pre-liquidation basis, the benefit appears to be more than a 10 percent (94.8 percent versus 84.3 percent) increase in tax efficiency when, in fact, the benefit is only 6 percent (84.0 percent versus 78.4 percent) as a result of the accumulation of capital gains in the Non-Large-Cap Swapped with TAA Portfolio. Taxes must be paid on these capital gains at liquidation.

Portfolio Drift

Portfolio drift is costly. A portfolio that begins with a 50/50 equity/fixed-income allocation will, if unchecked, shift gradually over time (portfolio drift) until the end result is a portfolio in which the risk has increased substantially more than the expected return. **Table 6** shows that for such a portfolio, the return per unit of risk falls dramatically as the time period stretches from 1 year (0.86) to 50 years (0.67). Allowing drift to continue unabated is not an efficient management approach. At the same time, rebalancing to stop portfolio drift carries with it the curse of the taxable investor—capital gains taxes. For this reason, derivatives strategies are extremely useful in managing individual investor portfolios because these strategies allow the manager to combat portfolio drift and some of the taxes arising from rebalancing the portfolio.

New Risks

Using derivatives exposes the investor to four categories of risk that the investor would not be exposed to with traditional physical securities. Thus, an approach using derivatives requires a careful review of potential risks.

Counterparty Risk. Anybody who suffered through the 1998 ruble crisis knows that a hedge is only as good as the counterparty to the trade because, in 1998, certain ruble counterparties did not stand behind their obligations. Therefore, managers must do sufficient due diligence to ascertain the creditworthiness of the counterparty before entering into a transaction. And particularly when they are running hybrid portfolios, managers need to practice counterparty exposure management.

Regulatory Risk. Using derivatives strategies creates substantial regulatory risks. Many of these strategies are so new that they have yet to be adequately IRS tested; investors, therefore, cannot be absolutely sure of their tax-treatment position. These strategies also come close to impinging on the straddle rules and the constructive sale/purchase rules, which also adds to potential regulatory and investment complications. Always check with an accountant or attorney before implementing any of these derivatives strategies.

Administrative Risk. The administrative risks from using derivatives arise from the complexity of

Table 6. Characteristics of a 50/50 Equity/Fixed Income Portfolio over Time

Measure	1 Year	3 Years	5 Years	10 Years	20 Years	50 Years
Risk (%)	11.6	11.8	12.1	12.6	13.6	16.1
Return (%)	10.0	10.0	10.1	10.2	10.3	10.8
Return per unit of risk	0.86	0.85	0.84	0.81	0.76	0.67

the strategies and the "lumpiness" of the contracts (i.e., contracts are typically available in large, set notional amounts and thus cannot always be customized to the specific need of the portfolio manager).

Because of the complexity of the strategies, the investor has to model risk carefully and test the model with all possible assumptions. (Model risk arises when managers forget to test for certain circumstances that they failed to make explicit.) Most real-world events do not fit a bell-shaped curve, so modeling behavior at the extremes—in the fat tails—is important in assessing the portfolio risk of a particular strategy. The complexity of the derivatives strategies also introduces accounting risk into the portfolio. Indeed, these derivatives strategies work best when they qualify for the IRC Section 1234 Rule, which liberates the investor from the mark-to-market rules—rules that require the investor to pay taxes annually on any gains even if the gain is only a paper gain. To qualify, the transactions must be private market transactions, but because they are private market transactions, the investor cannot look to the markets to independently value the transaction but must find a brokerage firm that will accurately value the instruments used in the transaction. The investor must thus know how to appropriately account for and report the transaction.

The contracts are also extremely lumpy. Executing a swap on a $10 million portfolio is much easier than on a $100,000 portfolio. So, for smaller investors, these strategies are extremely difficult to execute.

Investor Suitability Risk. Derivatives strategies are considerably more complex to explain to investors than are traditional strategies, and consequently, they are best suited to sophisticated investors. When a manager creates a hedge for an investor, the investor is both long a security and short a security, so the hedge will produce a loss on either the long side or the short side. The manager can only hope that the side that makes money will make more money than the losing side loses. I have seen clients become extremely upset when they discover that they have lost money on part of a strategy. Thus, the manager would be wise to make sure that the client has the ability to understand the strategy's consequences and, in particular, the ability to view all the various parts of the strategy as a single transaction. If the client is able to view the strategy in its entirety, the client will be able to gauge its success by the resulting overall gain or loss, after taxes, rather than by the individual profit and loss statements of each piece of the puzzle.

Conclusion

Derivatives can be used to enhance tax efficiency because they allow managers to control the timing of their execution decisions. With a portfolio of entirely physical securities, taxes are imposed when securities are sold. These securities are replaced with other securities, which may or may not produce an expected return that compensates for the tax paid on the securities sold to buy them. This outcome is particularly poignant when the assets sold either have a low tax basis or have substantially appreciated in value. Derivatives strategies allow the deferral of capital gains taxes arising from the rebalancing or repositioning of the portfolio and vastly increase management flexibility of portfolios.

Derivatives also allow managers to segregate the decision axis—security selection, strategic asset allocation, and portfolio rebalancing—and strategy implementation, which can enhance the after-tax alpha produced by a portfolio. But managers need to remember that with derivatives strategies come new portfolio risks—counterparty, regulatory, administrative, and investor suitability—that must be controlled carefully.

Question and Answer Session

Jean L.P. Brunel, CFA

Question: At what account value do these strategies begin to make sense, given their complexity and the transaction costs?

Brunel: When dealing with an individual security transaction, you can buy exchange-traded options in quantities of as little as 1,000 shares that trade for a few dollars; thus, a $500,000 account can certainly do individual option trading when appropriate. When dealing with a more complex segregation, the account probably needs to be in the $5 million and above range.

Question: How competitive is the pricing of derivatives among brokers, and how easy is it to shop around for the lowest cost?

Brunel: In talking about non-exchange-traded contracts, three things come into play. First, what is the book position of the dealer making the bid? If the dealer happens to have a natural position on the other side, he or she will quote a price that is considerably cheaper than one your best friend will quote. Unless you happen to have a direct line to that dealer, however, you will not be able to find that quote. Second is the issue of the negotiation of the documents. The documents are extremely thick with provisions for everything, including what happens if the firm is taken over and so forth. And then third is the follow up provided by the dealers in terms of providing you with inputs as to the value of the position on a day-to-day basis.

These derivatives strategies are not simple to do. I would argue that for investment firms that are part of a broader umbrella of companies and that can use a merchant banking or a brokerage arm within that umbrella to consummate the transaction, they will find these transactions easier to do. For others, I suggest hiring firms that are specialized in setting up these derivatives transactions, which does not mean hiring investment consultants because many of them are not naturally equipped to handle them.

Question: Is there any benefit to rebalancing more frequently than annually?

Brunel: Yes and no. With more frequent rebalancing, you are not only capturing the normal rebalancing; you are also aiming to capture some of the random volatility that occurs across various markets. I did some research with respect to styles that showed a benefit to monthly as opposed to annual rebalancing.[1] But the real issue in frequent rebalancing is that the more we trade, the more we expose ourselves to such issues as incurring wash sales and finding substitutable indexes so that we do not trigger the straddle rules. At some point, it just becomes too complex in relation to the benefit that is sought. There is value, there is alpha, but the alpha is hard to achieve. The friction costs are high for smaller portfolios.

My personal experience is that unless a dramatic event has occurred (and by dramatic, I mean the portfolio moves substantially more than 2–3 percent up or down in value in a short period of time), rebalancing does not make sense. Frankly, often a two- or three-year rebalancing cycle, as opposed to

---
[1] Jean L.P. Brunel, "Active Style Diversification in an After-Tax Context: An Impossible Challenge?" *Journal of Private Portfolio Management* (Spring 2000):41–50.

every year, provides the greatest benefit. And remember that if you are rebalancing with futures, the really liquid futures market is three months out, so you are effectively rebalancing quarterly.

Question: Why would someone want to intentionally trigger a wash sale, as in your example?

Brunel: Imagine for a minute that you have a loss that you want to take, but you also want to continue to own the security. The idea behind intentionally triggering the wash sale is that you are transferring the loss on the security that you sell to the basis of your option. But the whole purpose of the intentional wash-sale trade is to sell the option in two days' time. Thus, you considerably shorten the time frame of the wash sale, which normally is 31 days; with this strategy, it is 2 or 3 days. So, you trigger the wash-sale rule only for the benefit of being able to start another transaction that can be closed quickly; that is the whole of point of the strategy.

This strategy ought to be checked very carefully by your own accountants because certain accountants will advise you that you can basically undo the transaction the next day. If this is the case, the wash-sale waiting period drops from 31 days to 1 day, which is a great benefit. Yet other accountants will advise you to wait a week or two, in which case you will have to weigh the hassle factor against the risk inherent in this longer waiting period in order to shorten the wash-sale period only by about 15 days.

Question: What is tax-efficient large cap? Why is it tax efficient, and could you give an example?

Brunel: Tax efficiency can be achieved in three ways. One way is what such firms as Parametric Portfolio Associates and First Quadrant call "active tax management." It involves recognizing that active management is all about accepting tracking error for the purpose of realizing some gain. That gain can be in the form of having higher pretax return or better tax efficiency than the index. Thus, one tax-efficient strategy is active tax management.

Another tax-efficient strategy involves an optimizer, which allows the manager to capture as many analyst insights as possible within the context of a portfolio that does not allow trading *unless* the trade results in a net positive alpha. This is what we were doing at J.P. Morgan & Company.

A third possibility is Scudder Investments' approach. Instead of using a different portfolio construction process, Scudder uses a different research process in which it screens its stock universe by tilting the universe toward stocks that appear to have high tax efficiency built into them. These stocks tend to be classified as growth stocks and have fewer dividends. Scudder then scores these stocks and allows its portfolio managers to use a standard portfolio construction process applied to a universe that has been cleaned up of securities that have a greater chance for a tax-inefficient return.

The Diversification of Employee Stock Options

David M. Stein
Managing Director and Chief Investment Officer
Parametric Portfolio Associates
Seattle

Andrew F. Siegel
Professor of Finance and Management Science
University of Washington
Seattle

> Employee options offer large potential wealth, but they come with the risk of overexposure to the employer's stock. A disciplined framework for deciding how many options to exercise and sell as a function of other wealth, the stock price, the time to expiration, and other parameters can help employee optionholders manage their risks while still retaining the possibility of large upside gains.

Many companies compensate their employees with call options on their stock. Such employees have the potential to build a great deal of wealth in their employers' stock, but this opportunity comes with the risk of concentration. For example, many employees of Microsoft Corporation have accumulated significant wealth in Microsoft options. They have bought houses near Redmond, WA; they may have retirement plans heavily invested in Microsoft stock; and they may have spouses who work for Seattle companies that are sensitive to the regional economy. Their exposure to Microsoft's financial performance is high, and if Microsoft's stock price drops, the financial repercussions can be severe.

We have spoken and written about the diversification of concentrated wealth before.[1] Much of tax management is concerned with reducing or deferring a tax liability, but one needs to understand when to defer taxes and when not to. With concentrated risk, it is often desirable to simply diversify, bite the tax bullet, and then move forward in a tax-efficient way.

In this presentation, we discuss employee options in the context of concentrated wealth. We give a short introduction to employee options and their taxation. Then, we present a simplified problem of nonqualified, nonrestricted employee options and solve for when to exercise and sell. As is typical for options in general, the solution is fairly complex. Nevertheless, our analysis provides a framework for understanding the problem and determining a decision strategy.

Option-pricing theory, which is well known, loved, and studied by academics and practitioners, cannot be used directly to solve our problem for two reasons. First, most option-pricing theory does not include taxes, and taxes are a significant factor in financial decision making. Second, and more important, an employee option cannot be sold. It can only be exercised, which means that when the employee exercises the option, she loses its time value. A large focus of option-pricing theory is the determination of time value.

What drives the employee to hold an option rather than to exercise? The answer is that she wants to retain the upside potential of the stock rather than discard it. Also, she is eager to defer the tax bill as long as possible.

---

[1] See David M. Stein, "Diversification of Highly Concentrated Portfolios in the Presence of Taxes," *Investment Counseling for Private Clients II* (Charlottesville, VA: AIMR, 2000):18–25; David M. Stein, Andrew F. Siegel, Premkumar Narasimhan, and Charles E. Appeadu, "Diversification in the Presence of Taxes," *Journal of Portfolio Management* (Fall 2000):61–71.

Editor's note: This material was presented at the conference solely by Mr. Stein.

But options are risky. An option position is, in a sense, like a leveraged position in the underlying stock. As the stock price moves, the rate of return of the option fluctuates more than the underlying stock price, particularly if the option is near to or out of the money. If the option is well in the money (the stock price has risen well above the strike price), it behaves somewhat like a long position in the stock.

Adding complexity is the fact that the employee typically receives numerous grants of options over time, and grants are often subject to vesting restrictions.

Taxation of Employee Options[2]

On exercise of an option, the employee acquires the underlying stock by paying the strike price. At this point, the employee can hold the stock (exercise and hold) or sell the stock (exercise and sell). Exercising the option triggers a tax event, and the taxes depend on the type of option.

Employee options are either nonqualified (NQ) options or incentive stock options (ISOs). For NQ options, the intrinsic value of the option (stock price minus strike price) is taxed at ordinary income tax rates. For a typical highly compensated employee, the applicable income tax rate (federal plus state) is often more than 40 percent.[3] The tax is the same whether or not the employee holds the stock. If the employee holds the stock, the cost basis of the holding is its value at exercise; taxes have already been paid.

For NQ options, exercise and hold is the same as exercise and sell with a subsequent repurchase of the stock. If the employee continues to hold the stock, she pays taxes and still incurs the concentration risk, which does not make much sense unless she is extremely confident that the stock price will increase. For NQ options, the undiversified employee should instead exercise and sell immediately.

ISOs are slightly different from NQ options, and their structure and analysis are more complex. Under certain circumstances, the intrinsic value on exercise of an ISO is taxed as a capital gain rather than as ordinary income. To obtain this beneficial tax treatment, the employee must exercise the option and hold the stock for at least one year; the cost basis is set to the exercise price, and when the stock is sold in the future, any gain is taxed at the capital gains rate. If the employee sells the stock without holding it the full year, the intrinsic value is taxed at the ordinary income tax rate (i.e., taxation is like that of a NQ option).

Taxation of ISOs is further complicated because the gain on exercise is viewed as an alternative minimum tax (AMT) "preference item," which could effectively increase the tax rate.

Simplified Problem

The analytical question we pose is when should an employee exercise and sell a holding of NQ options that have no restrictions and are fully vested. As mentioned, exercise and hold is not a useful strategy if the risk is one of concentration.

If the option is out of the money (the stock price is below the strike price), the employee should hold the option because the employee has nothing to gain by exercising it. If the option is well in the money (the stock price has risen well above the strike price), the employee can think of the option as being a long stock position on which taxes are due.[4]

We assume that the options are a large portion of the employee's wealth. The employee has other wealth in an indexed diversified stock market portfolio. The employee exercises and sells a portion of the options and pays the taxes due. After exercising, the employee invests the proceeds in the same indexed investment.

At each point, the simplified portfolio consists of two assets: a holding of unexercised options and a holding of a diversified stock market position. Decisions will depend on the amount of money in each of these assets and the time to maturity of the options as well as the price of the underlying stock, tax rates, and so on.

A given decision strategy for exercising options will result in an outcome at the end of an investment horizon. The outcome of final wealth is uncertain and depends on how the stock price moves. We assume a lognormal stochastic process for the stock price movements, which allows us to simulate the probability distribution of final wealth for this decision strategy. We compare decision-making strategies by comparing the probability distributions of final wealth that they generate.

Without a loss in generality, we assume that the option strike price is $100. To fix ideas further, in the numerical examples that follow, we set additional parameters: The volatility of the underlying stock is 40 percent (this number is comparable to the volatility of IBM); the return expectations for both the stock market and the stock are 8 percent a year; the stock's beta is 1; the stock market has a volatility of 15 percent; tax rates are 20 percent on capital gains and 40

---

[2] Note that our discussion of the taxation of options is simplified for expositional and analytical purposes. Please see a tax advisor for tax advice.

[3] Taxes are often withheld on exercise.

[4] A subindustry has emerged to hedge concentrated risk with variable prepaid forwards and other hedging strategies, but discussion of this topic is beyond our scope here.

percent on ordinary income; and the investor's investment horizon is 20 years from the time the options were granted, at which time all holdings are liquidated. Of course, in our more general analysis, these settings are all parameterized.

Case 1: Initial Wealth at Time 0 and No Other Wealth. On Day 1 at the beginning of the 20-year investment period, the employee is awarded a grant of options. At this time, the underlying stock price is $100, the strike price is $100, and the time to expiration is 10 years. The employee has no other wealth, only the options.

If the employee decides to hold the options to expiration, exercising when they expire in 10 years' time and investing in a diversified stock market portfolio that grows at the expected rate of 8 percent a year for the second 10-year period, what can he expect to have after taxes at the horizon? We determine this amount by simulating 10,000 Monte Carlo scenarios, each a path of stock price movements. The resulting distribution of final wealth is shown in the histogram of **Figure 1**. The horizon expected value is $163, and the median value is only $13. The probability of ending with nothing is 46 percent: The employee has close to an even chance (46 percent) that his options will expire worthless, even under the assumption that both the market and the stock will return 8 percent a year. Note that he also has a good chance of doing extremely well.

Case 2: Five Years Later and Some Other Wealth. It is now five years after the initial grant, and the stock price is $125. The employee has other wealth invested in the market, and the options are roughly half the employee's total pretax wealth at this time. That is, for each $25 in intrinsic option value, he has another $25 in a diversified stock market portfolio. (In the analysis, we also need to know the cost basis of this stock market portfolio, so we set it to be 75 percent of market value.)

Once again, suppose that he holds the options to expiration and then combines their after-tax value with his appreciated market holdings for the remaining period. We can again simulate his final wealth 15 years later at the end of the original 20-year period; the distribution of final after-tax wealth is shown in **Figure 2**. In this case, the employee can expect his $50 today ($25 in intrinsic option value and $25 in a diversified portfolio) to have grown to $182. There is a 50 percent likelihood that the $50 grows to $104 or more. The standard deviation, a measure of the uncertainty of the distribution, is $248; the distribution is fairly broad and uncertain.

Consider what happens if he exercises the options. The strike price is $100, and the pretax

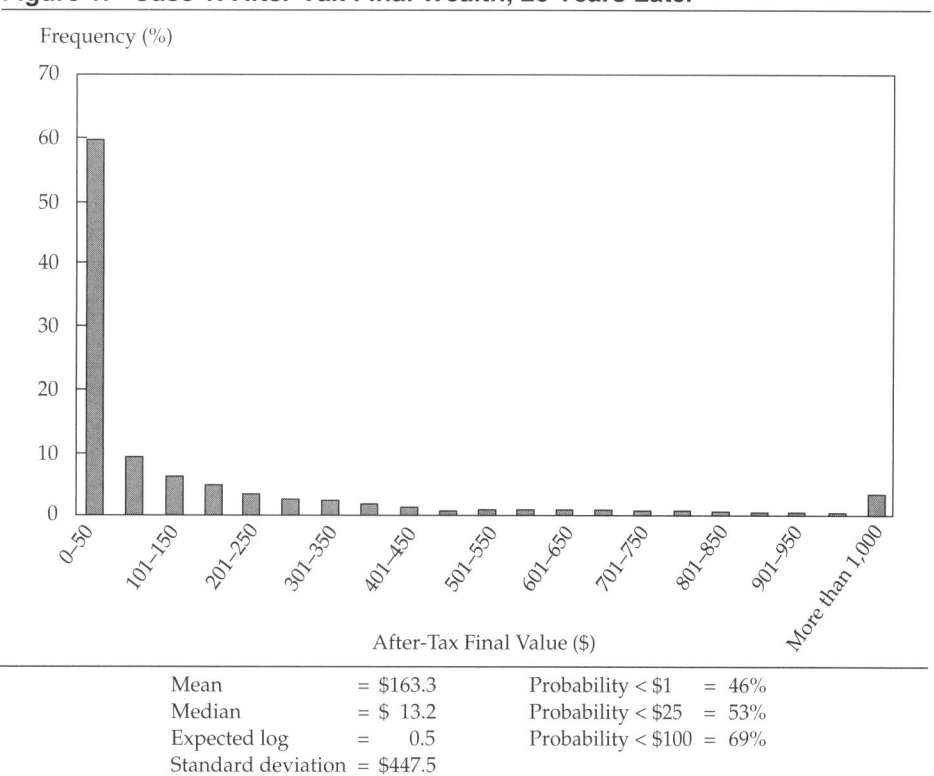

Figure 1. Case 1: After-Tax Final Wealth, 20 Years Later

Mean	= $163.3	Probability < $1	= 46%
Median	= $ 13.2	Probability < $25	= 53%
Expected log	= 0.5	Probability < $100	= 69%
Standard deviation	= $447.5		

Figure 2. Case 2: After-Tax Final Wealth: No Options Exercised

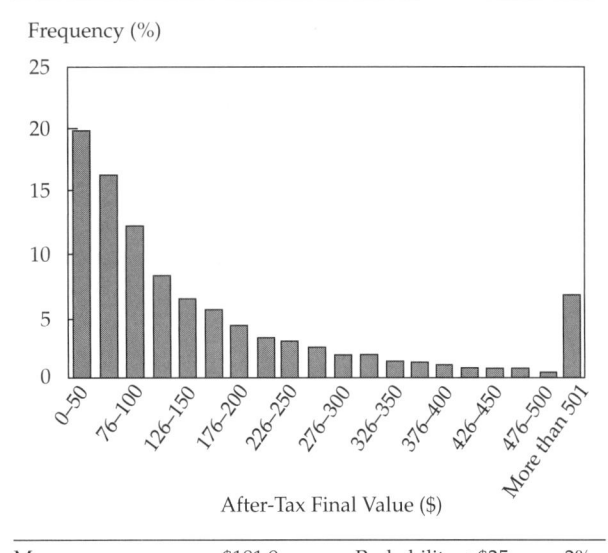

Mean	= $181.9	Probability < $25	= 2%
Median	= $104.4	Probability < $50	= 20%
Expected log	= 4.7	Probability < $100	= 49%
Standard deviation	= $248.5		

intrinsic value of each exercised option is $25. After paying ordinary income taxes of 40 percent on the option value, he is left with $15 from each option, which he invests in the market for the remaining time to the horizon's end (15 years). The resulting distribution is that of **Figure 3**. His horizon expectation is

Figure 3. Case 2: After-Tax Final Wealth: All Options Exercised

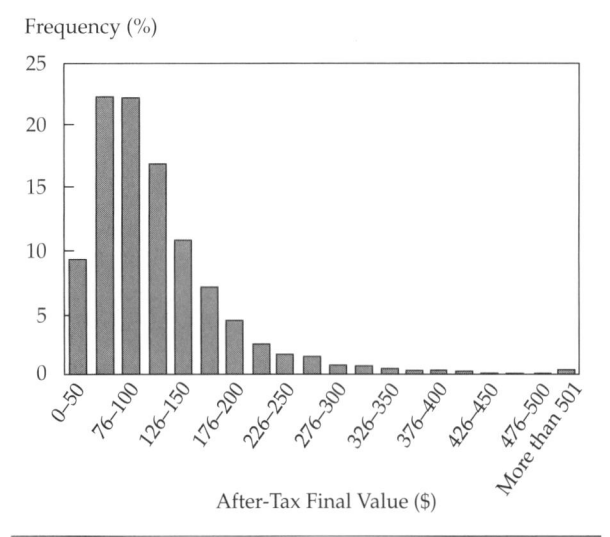

Mean	= $108.9	Probability < $25	= 0%
Median	= $ 95.1	Probability < $50	= 9%
Expected log	= 4.6	Probability < $100	= 54%
Standard deviation	= $ 59.6		

now $109, substantially lower than before, but the distribution is more certain. The employee has forgone the upside potential of the options. The larger upside in Figure 2 is attributable to the options rather than the diversified stock portfolio, so he has lowered his risk by exercising the options.

Which of these choices (holding until expiration or exercising now at the five-year point) is preferable? To some people, not exercising looks more attractive. Between the two extremes is a decision to exercise 20 percent of the options, holding the rest to expiration. The resulting distribution is shown in **Figure 4**. In this case, the expected final value is $167. The median final wealth value of $106 is close to the median value of the no-exercise strategy, but the employee still maintains a large portion of the upside potential.

Figure 4. Case 2: After-Tax Final Wealth: 20 Percent of Options Exercised

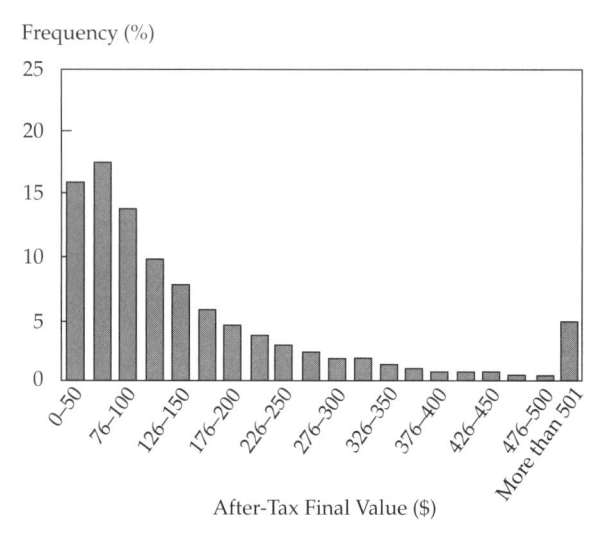

Mean	= $167.3	Probability < $25	= 1%
Median	= $106.0	Probability < $50	= 16%
Expected log	= 4.7	Probability < $100	= 47%
Standard deviation	= $204.7		

Comparing Distributions of Final Wealth. Which decision is best in Case 2? To answer this question, we need to make a trade-off between risk and return among the horizon distributions. In previous work, we evaluated a risk-adjusted annualized return measure—the Sharpe ratio—for making this trade-off.[5] We focus now instead on end-of-period wealth and seek the decision that maximizes the expected log of final wealth—that is,

$$E(w) = \frac{[\ln(w_1) + \ln(w_2) + \ldots + \ln(w_n)]}{n}.$$

[5] Stein, Siegel, Narasimhan, and Appeadu, *op. cit.*

This utility function prefers any strategy that increases wealth with little or no risk. And, as academics like to say, it is risk averse with a constant relative risk aversion. One can think of the horizon wealth as a compounded annual return, so maximizing this utility maximizes the growth rate. This approach has a powerful attribute: It is growth optimal. Over the long run, an investor who is focused on maximizing this expected log utility function does at least as well as any other investor who chooses another strategy.

Decision Strategies: Static. At the five-year point in Case 2, what is the investor's best static strategy? We must recognize that the decision examples we have discussed are examples of what we call a "static" strategy: A decision is made now, and future decisions do not change based on how the future unfolds. In a few moments, we will extend this notion. For Case 2, it turns out that the best static decision—the one that maximizes the expected log value—is to exercise about 15 percent of the options, close to the case of Figure 4.

Figure 5 generalizes the optimal static decision in a number of dimensions. First, we fix the amount of other wealth by assuming in this figure that the intrinsic value of the options constitutes half the employee's wealth at the decision point.[6] The lines in Figure 5 show the optimal static decision—the proportion of options to exercise—as a function of the stock price and the options' time to expiration.

Figure 5. Static Decision: Amount to Exercise When Options Are Half Pretax Wealth

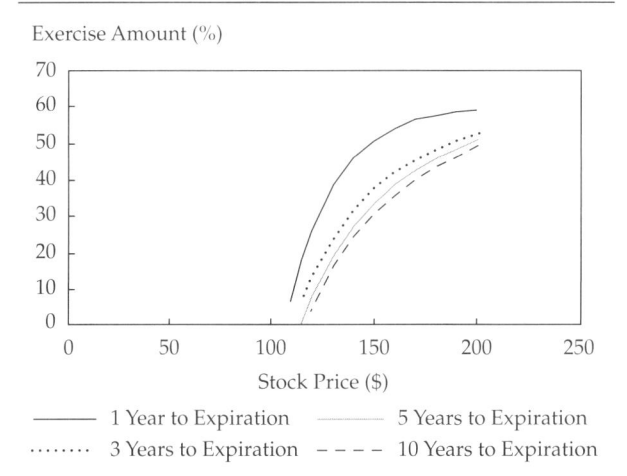

When the stock price is high (i.e., when the options are well in the money), the employee will

[6]For example, when the pretax intrinsic value of the options is $1,000, the other wealth (all in a diversified stock market portfolio) is also $1,000. We again set the cost basis of this wealth to be 75 percent of its market value.

want to exercise more than when the stock price is low. Similarly, if time to expiration is short (holding all other variables the same), then it is optimal to exercise more than when time to expiration is long. Following is our intuition: The time value of the options, which is lost on exercise, is low when either the underlying stock price is high (assuming the options are in the money) or the time is short.

Decision Strategies: Dynamic. Institutional money managers often use a myopic strategy: They make a current decision based on current forecasted returns and volatilities. This myopic strategy is often appropriate because few investors reason as follows: "I will be making a decision now, tomorrow, and next year, so my current decision will set me up for subsequent ones." But when taxes and other expenses are involved, as in our formulated problem with options, a current decision does affect future decision-making possibilities. Once an employee exercises many of his options, he cannot change his mind, so an alternative decision-making framework is useful prior to the exercise decision.

Consider again Case 2, five years after the award. An alternative strategy would be to continue to hold the options for the present and then to revisit this decision next year. A "dynamic" strategy takes into consideration the fact that a decision will be made at each period (in our simplified case, each year); the optimal dynamic strategy seeks the best decision now with the ability to make optimal decisions in the future as well.

Dynamic decision-making strategies are well known in operations research and industrial engineering where they are used to solve a wide variety of logistical problems. The solution method is that of dynamic programming's backward induction. For example, because the options expire in Year 10, in Year 9, the decision is to exercise at that point or to wait until Year 10, a static decision. We can solve for this best decision in Year 9 as a function of the stock price and the concentration. Next, we think about Year 8, and because we know how to make the decision in Year 9, we can determine what the employee should do in Year 8. We work backwards until we find the optimal decision at the initial time.

This mathematical process is fairly complex. It requires backward induction on a multidimensional grid. Our grid state is defined by the stock price, strike price, time to expiration, value of other wealth, cost basis of other wealth at each point in time, and the number of option contracts held. Computation is intensive, and in the end, it produces the optimal amount to exercise and sell as a function of the state at each point in time. And as one might expect, compared with the optimal static decision, the optimal dynamic decision depends on how far in the money the options are and on the amount of other wealth. When the options are near the money and there is a long time before expiration, the optimal dynamic decision differs from the static one. As one might expect, the dynamic decision delays the rate at which the options are exercised. When the options are well in the money (more than about 1.5 times the strike price), the dynamic decision is similar to the static decision.

So, what would the dynamic decision be for the earlier simple example of Case 2? Recall that the optimal static decision was to exercise about 15 percent of the options. The best dynamic decision delays exercising the options but revisits the question each year in the future. With our simulated scenarios, we use the optimal dynamic decision and obtain the distribution of final wealth of **Figure 6**. Compared with the static decision (Figure 4), the expected log increases,[7] as does the median. The uncertainty decreases (i.e., the probability of doing poorly drops substantially), and the probability of doing well increases.

Figure 6. Case 2: After-Tax Final Wealth: Dynamic Decision

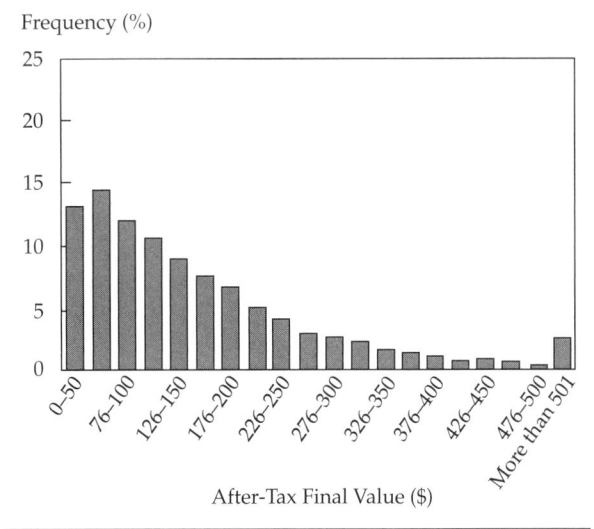

Mean	= $160.1	Probability < $25	= 1%
Median	= $123.9	Probability < $50	= 13%
Expected log	= 4.8	Probability < $100	= 40%
Standard deviation	= $131.5		

The more general question of how much to exercise using a dynamic strategy is again complex. A graph showing the optimal dynamic decision (and corresponding to the static one of Figure 5) is shown in **Figure 7**. Note, again, for this figure we are fixing

[7] Note that the expected utility is on a logarithmic scale; a small increase makes a large difference.

Figure 7. Dynamic Decision: Amount to Exercise When Options Are Half Pretax Wealth

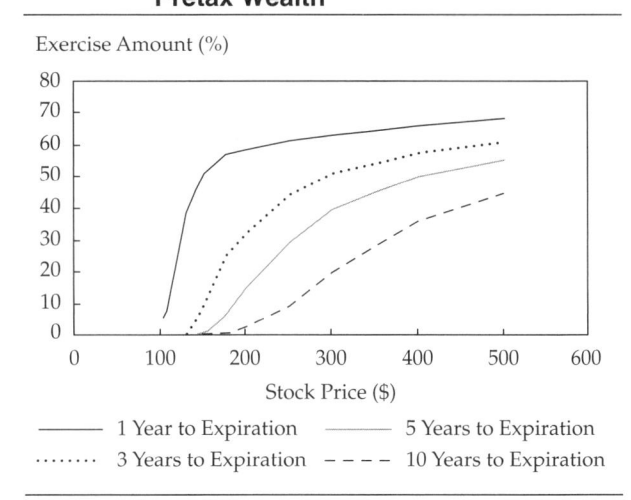

the amount of other wealth by assuming that the options constitute half the total pretax wealth. With five years to go before expiration and the underlying stock price of $125, the employee would not exercise any options. But if the underlying stock price were $200 with five years before expiration, he would exercise 15 percent of the options. And if the stock price were $300, he would exercise 40 percent. If the time before expiration is longer, say 10 years, and the stock price is $200 (and the options still constitute half his wealth), he would exercise less so as to retain the time value of the options. Comparing Figure 5 with Figure 7, the one-year-to-go cases are the same: Our dynamic process makes a decision each year, and the decision in Year 9 is a static one.

Examples

Let us apply our dynamic decision to two examples: an IBM employee and an Amazon.com employee.

IBM Employee. Suppose an IBM employee was awarded 100 options at a strike price (split adjusted) of $22.40 in January 1992 with a 10-year expiration. Suppose that she has other wealth at this time of $560 in a stock market index, with a cost basis of $420.[8]

The solid heavy line in **Figure 8** shows the stock price movement of IBM during the subsequent 10-year period, and the dashed line shows the scaled performance of the S&P 500 Index. IBM outperformed the S&P 500 during the period. The thin solid lines show when the employee would have exercised the options based on our dynamic process, taking into account her other wealth. Until about 1996, when

[8] We are taking 25 percent of the 100 options times a $22.40 strike price with a cost basis equal to 75 percent of market value.

Figure 8. IBM Options: Dynamic Exercise

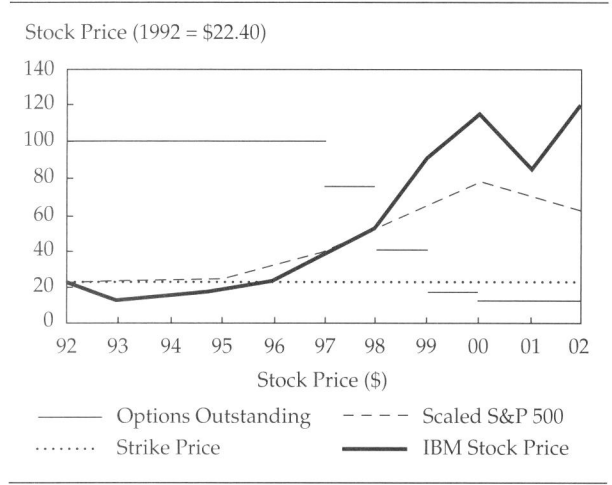

the IBM options were out of the money, the employee would have continued to hold them. But when the IBM stock price recovered and reached about $40 in 1997, the employee would have exercised about 25 percent of the options. Over the 10-year period, the employee would have gradually exercised the options until only a few remained in 2002, when they were finally exercised.

How well did this strategy do? The employee started with $560 in other wealth and the 100 options, and at the end of the period, her total wealth grew to about $4,500, as shown in **Table 1**. Had the employee held the options to expiration, her final wealth would have been roughly $6,000. Exercising the options resulted in less wealth because IBM's stock price continued to rise steadily after exercise, exceeding returns on the S&P 500. Although in retrospect holding the options would have been preferable, this result does not mean that holding the options would have been a sensible decision to make. The risk involved would have been high.[9] Compared with other possible decisions, this employee did well.

Amazon Employee. Suppose in 1998 an Amazon employee was awarded 100 stock options that expire in 10 years with a strike price of $4.96. He also had other wealth at this time of $124 in a stock market index, with a cost basis of $93. **Figure 9** shows how Amazon's stock price rose in the period from 1998 to 2000. When the stock price reached about $60 in 1999, our dynamic strategy would have suggested that the employee exercise a substantial proportion of his options, about 98 percent. The amount exercised is high because of the huge price appreciation on Amazon stock and the now serious concentration risk. The next year, the stock price was even higher, and once again, the dynamic strategy would have exercised about another 1 percent of the options. As **Table 2** shows, this employee's total 1998 wealth of $124 plus options would have grown to roughly $3,200 at the end of the five-year period. Had the employee held the options, riding Amazon's stock price up and back again down, he would have ended with approximately $360 in total wealth at the end of 2001. In this case, the employee did well by exercising the options. But observe that this story is not yet over because it is (faintly) conceivable that Amazon will yet recover to its previous highs before the option expiration in 2008.

Figure 9. Amazon: Dynamic Exercise

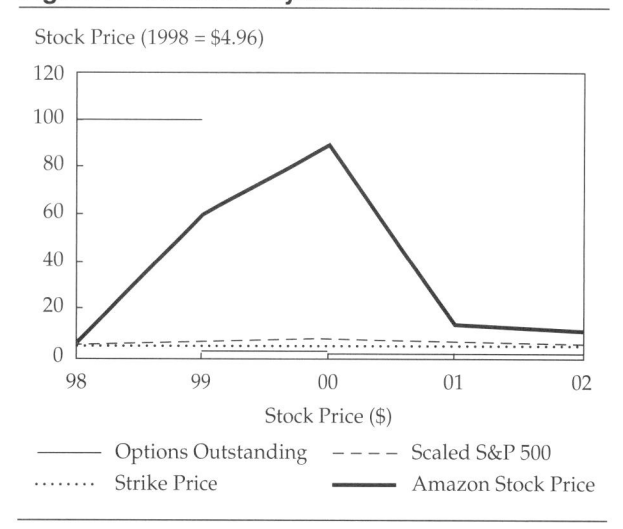

Table 1. IBM Options: Dynamic Exercise

Date	Number of Options	Wealth in Market	Cost Basis
1992	100.0	$ 559	$ 419
1993	100.0	583	419
1994	100.0	624	419
1995	100.0	615	419
1996	100.0	832	419
1997	75.2	1,223	655
1998	40.7	2,249	1,286
1999	17.1	3,816	2,269
2000	12.6	4,775	2,522
2001	12.5	4,212	2,524
2002	0.0	4,546	3,279

If all options exercised in January 2002
| January 2002 | | 6,028 | 6,028 |

Conclusion

Employee options offer large potential wealth, but unless they are managed carefully, their potential may evaporate. Managing options requires a disciplined strategy—one that evaluates the employee's position

---
[9] Between January and April 2002, IBM dropped 31 percent, substantially underperforming the S&P 500, which dropped 6 percent.

Table 2. Amazon: Dynamic Exercise

Date	Number of Options	Amount in Market	Cost Basis
1998	100.0	$ 124	$ 93
1999	2.4	3,377	3,314
2000	1.4	4,054	3,366
2001	1.4	3,575	3,366
2002	0.0	3,222	3,371

If all options exercised in January 2002

| January 2002 | | 366 | 366 |

at each point in time to determine how much to exercise and sell. In this presentation, we have introduced a dynamic framework for making this decision, one that incorporates taxes, the fraction of the employee's wealth that the options constitute, the price of the stock, the time to expiration, and other parameters.

Concentrated option positions are risky. Many investors and employees have suffered financially during the past years as their employers' stock has dropped. With careful decision making, employee optionholders can manage their risks while still retaining the possibility of large upside gains.

Question and Answer Session
David M. Stein

Question: You have done some involved analysis and computations in your presentation. Can any of this information be "ball parked"?

Stein: Yes and no. I think Figures 5 and 7 capture the decision making quite nicely. Certainly, when I write this up in detail,[10] I'll offer more examples and show what happens, for instance, when the fraction of other wealth isn't 50 percent. And yet in formulating a simplified problem, we do not want to lose its essence. If you discard the stochastic analysis, then you discard the meat of the problem.

The question is how an employee should make the decision to exercise options over time as the stock price and the employee's total wealth change. Unfortunately, the decision-making process cannot be easily applied to a wide range of people who hold options because each case depends on numerous parameters—stock price, time to expiration, other wealth. It is hard at this time for us to present the results in a simple and easy-to-use form. It is also hard to do the computations, although we are working on simplifying them. If you have ideas on how to do this, I'd love to hear them.

Question: Does the decision whether to exercise depend largely on the relative return and volatility expectations of the underlying stock and the other wealth?

Stein: Yes, the results do depend on return and volatility assumptions of the underlying stock.

If you have a high expected alpha on the stock compared with the market, you would diversify more slowly. But (as with the single-stock case) you need to make heroic assumptions to justify not diversifying. Of course, if you are convinced that the stock has large alpha, hold the stock. As an advisor to such an investor, I would push the investor to articulate why he or she is so convinced that this stock is underpriced and will do so well in the face of market competition.

Similarly, if the volatility of the stock is higher, you will want to diversify more. For simplicity, most of our analysis here assumes a volatility of 40 percent. In the Amazon example, we assumed a volatility of 80 percent.

---
[10] A more detailed paper is in preparation to be published.

Strategies for Retirement Benefits in Estate Planning

Natalie B. Choate
Of Counsel
Bingham Dana LLP
Boston

> For a number of reasons having mostly to do with demographics and changing tax laws, advisors will soon find themselves with an increasing number of clients who want to set up estate plans for their retirement benefits and/or who are the beneficiaries of inherited plans. Although knowing the advantages of the life expectancy payout is important, familiarity with the intricacies of distribution calculations, tax laws, plan transfer rules, and charitable strategies is vital to protecting these clients' assets and ensuring compliance with the law.

In this presentation, I will start by discussing the importance of having strategies in place for handling retirement benefits in an estate plan. I will then go into quite a bit of detail on how to handle a pre-owned IRA or retirement plan, and finally, I will look at using charitable strategies with retirement benefits. More information on all these issues can be found in *Life and Death Planning for Retirement Benefits*.[1]

Importance of Planning

Estate planning for retirement benefits is becoming increasingly important for investment professionals and estate-planning professionals largely because of three reasons. The first two reasons can be primarily attributed to recent changes related to retirement plans: More money is going into these plans, and money can remain in them much longer. The third reason is demographics.

More Money. More money is going into retirement plans. On June 7, 2001, the new tax law (the Economic Growth and Tax Relief Reconciliation Act of 2001) was signed into law. This new tax law has increased the amount of money that can go into retirement plans across the board. In some cases, the increase is substantial. For example, the limit for IRA contributions had been $2,000 a year for quite a long time. Starting in 2002, the maximum annual contribution has been increased to $3,000, and that amount will be scaled up over the next few years until it reaches $5,000 a year in 2008. In addition, people older than 50 by the end of 2002 can contribute an extra $500, and that extra amount for those older than 50 will go up to $1,000 a year in a few years. So, people older than 50 but younger than 70½ in 2002 can contribute as much as $3,500 to an IRA for themselves, depending on their compensation income.

Note that, theoretically, the IRA contribution has to come from income classified as compensation. Some people look at this situation and think that the tax-free buildup inside retirement plans is such a great deal that they want their children to benefit from it. If a child has a summer job or an after-school job and earns at least $3,000 during the year, then ostensibly a parent can set up an IRA (maybe even a Roth IRA, whose contributions are not tax deductible but whose distributions are) for the child and make a $3,000 contribution to the IRA for that year. But do not push it. For example, someone told me he wanted to set up an IRA for his child because he thought these tax-deferred retirement plans are a great deal. Because the child was only five years old, she did not actually have a job, but she was required to keep her room clean. This person figured he could pay her $2,000 a year (at that time) to keep her room clean so that she would have compensation income to put into

---
[1] Natalie B. Choate, *Life and Death Planning for Retirement Benefits*, 4th ed. (Boston, MA: Ataxplan Publications, 2002). To obtain a copy of this book, call 800-247-6553 or go to www.ataxplan.com.

an IRA. The problem is that the fund contribution must legitimately come from compensation income; a gift is not compensation. If the U.S. IRS decides this five-year-old child did not earn this money and it was merely a gift, then the parent is not starting her off with a fabulous retirement nest egg. He is starting her off with criminal penalties and an IRS record, which is not a good way to start life. Therefore, do not get carried away by the lure of IRAs.

For 401(k) plans (a particular type of defined-contribution plan), the maximum that could be contributed was $10,500 in 2001. For 2002, it is $11,000. That amount is scheduled to go up to $15,000 in the next few years. Again, people who will be older than 50 by the end of the calendar year will get an extra add-on of $1,000 in 2002 and all subsequent years. Although these older-than-50 provisions were designed to help women older than 50 save for retirement, as enacted, anybody can use them.

Retirement plans for businesses were also given an increase in the maximum contribution limit, which is of special interest to executives and small business owners. Keep in mind that a defined-benefit plan is a plan that promises the employee that a certain annual pension will be available at retirement. Whereas the contribution for defined-contribution plans can be either a fixed dollar amount or a certain percentage of the employees' pay, the contribution for a defined-benefit plan is the amount the employer has to put into the fund based on the promise made to himself or his employee(s), whatever that amount may be. In 2001, the maximum retirement benefit that could be funded was $140,000 a year, starting at age 65. In 2002, the most that can be funded is an annual fixed pension of $160,000 a year for life, starting at age 62. A pension of $160,000 a year is an expensive promise to fund, and the small business owner may need to set aside well over $100,000 a year, tax deductible, just to meet this pension promise to himself.

Congress is worried that not enough money is being saved for retirement and that more money should go into plans. For the investment advisor, these changes in the tax law mean that the amount of money being contributed to retirement plans will grow.

More Time. Recent changes in the IRS's required distribution rules now allow money to remain in plans longer. Although a retirement plan is a wonderful tax-free investment vehicle, the downside is that when the money comes out of retirement plans (except for Roth IRAs), it is taxed at the taxpayer's current marginal tax rate, which results in planning difficulties at the individual taxpayer level. Congress has said that the money cannot stay in this tax-free environment forever and has established so-called minimum distribution rules that specify when the money has to be withdrawn and taxed.

The minimum distribution rules apply to two conditions, life and death. I will discuss the lifetime rules here and address the death rules in a later section. When an individual hits 70½, he or she must start taking annual distributions out of the retirement plan. In 2001, the IRS changed the system for how those distributions are calculated. Under the new system, money can stay in the plan much longer than it could under the old system. Prior to 2001, reaching age 70½ meant the beginning of the end for the retirement plan because the person would have had to start taking distributions. Under the previous IRS rules, the distributions were so large early in the withdrawal period that in many cases by the time the person was 90 years old, the retirement plan assets were virtually depleted. But since the beginning of 2001, the situation is totally different. Now, the minimum distribution rules are so flexible that the individual is guaranteed never to deplete the assets in the retirement plan if the distributions begin at age 70½, provided the person takes only the minimum required distribution and does not have major investment losses.

For example, consider a client, Wilma, who is 70½ years old and has a $1 million IRA. Because Wilma must start taking distributions out of her IRA, she takes the minimum distribution, pays tax on it, and deposits the remainder in her checking account. The first year's distribution is only about 4 percent of the value of the IRA. The minimum distributions under the new rules are so small that the account will not fall below $1 million until Wilma reaches age 89 (assuming an investment return of 6 percent). No longer does turning 70½ imply the end of someone's retirement planning. In the new environment, assets can potentially stay in a plan for the client's entire life.

Demographics. The final factor that is making retirement planning more important is demographics, namely the aging of the Baby Boomer population. These people who are turning 50 at the rate of millions a day are suddenly waking up to the fact that they have not saved enough for retirement. Their free-spending ways are catching up with them. Many of these people who thought they were going to retire early are finding they cannot. Even some people who have already retired are suddenly discovering they have to go back to work because they do not have enough money to sustain their standard of living.

Pre-Owned IRAs

This section will not focus on the effects of IRA distributions on a client who is about to retire but, rather, on a new client who has just inherited an IRA.

Throughout this discussion, consider two things: planning and compliance. Investment advisors are always looking for planning opportunities—ways to help a client make and save money—but they are also looking at compliance obligations to prevent the client from getting stuck with penalties.

Advantages of Life Expectancy Payout. One of the first issues an advisor should explain to a client is something that the client may not have heard before—the advantages of the life expectancy payout method for retirement plans after death. The initial reaction of most clients who have inherited an IRA is that the account should be liquidated immediately and reinvested. When the client cashes out the plan, however, income taxes must be paid on the withdrawal.

Luckily, Congress has provided an option for heirs not to have to cash out right away. An heir is entitled to withdraw assets from an inherited IRA over his or her life expectancy, which can be found in IRS tables. Every year, a minimum required distribution, using a formula based on the remainder of the heir's life expectancy and the account balance, must be taken. Minimum required distributions are always based on an account balance divided by a life expectancy factor.

Suppose a new client whose father died October 30, 2001, appears in her investment advisor's office seeking advice. The advisor explains the life expectancy payout method, and the client says, "That sounds kind of complicated, why would I bother?" To illustrate why, the advisor could show her the difference (financially) between cashing out the IRA in a lump sum and taking the minimum required distributions over her life expectancy. The second alternative allows the assets remaining in the inherited IRA to continue to grow tax deferred. If the client (the beneficiary of the IRA) is 39 years old, the IRS attributes to her a life expectancy of an additional 44.6 years. The financial advantage to her in leaving as many assets in the IRA as possible and choosing to take only the minimum required distributions over the next 44.6 years is that at the end of those 44.6 years, the client will have more than twice the assets than if she cashed out the entire inherited IRA, paid income taxes on the proceeds, and invested in a taxable environment for those 44.6 years. Certainly, the financial advantage depends on the individual's tax bracket and where and how the money is invested. But by and large, leaving the assets in the tax-deferred environment of the IRA and withdrawing them over the heir's life expectancy is financially preferable to withdrawing all of the IRA assets at one time.

Annual Distribution Calculation. Suppose the advisor has convinced the client of the advantages of the life expectancy payout. Now the client says, "How do we calculate my annual distributions?" Some advisors find that doing this annual calculation for the client provides a good excuse for getting together with the client every year, updating the portfolio, and keeping in close contact with the client. In this way, compliance can work together with planning. Taking over the compliance for required distributions is a major service the investment advisor can perform for that client. And taking on this responsibility provides a payback for the advisor in the form of client satisfaction and maintaining a relationship with the client. The advisor, however, does not have to do the calculation. The client's accountant or attorney can do the calculation. Nevertheless, in my opinion, the advisor is in the best position to do the calculation because the advisor is closest to the account's balance.

- *Account balance.* The first piece of information that is needed, no matter who is doing the calculation, is the prior year-end account balance. In this case, the client's father died in 2001, so the December 31, 2001, account balance is the starting point for determining the required distribution for 2002.

- *Life expectancy.* The life expectancy factor is also needed for the required minimum distribution calculation. This information is given in the IRS life expectancy tables in IRS Publication 590, which is available to anyone for free. Note that final minimum distribution regulations issued by the IRS in April 2002 provided a new set of even more favorable tables than the ones included in the 2001 changes; these tables will not appear in Publication 590 until the 2003 edition. In this case, the client is 39 years old because she will be 39 at the end of the calendar year in which the first required minimum distribution will be made (in this case 2002). According to the IRS life expectancy tables, her life expectancy is 44.6 years, meaning that she is expected to live another 44.6 years beyond her current age.

- *The formula.* With the account balance from the prior year-end (2001), the age that the client will be at the end of the current year (2002), and the IRS life expectancy tables, the first year's required distribution amount can be calculated. The required distribution is the account balance divided by the life expectancy factor. The beneficiary has to take that amount out of the inherited IRA by the end of the year. The following year, the calculation is even simpler because the IRS tables are no longer needed. Each year's life expectancy factor is just the prior year's factor minus one. Keep in mind, however, that in the following year, the new account balance as of the prior year-end must be used.

■ *Caveats.* Calculating the required distribution does not appear difficult, but from time to time complications arise. For example, in April 2002 the IRS issued final minimum distribution regulations that allow IRA owners and beneficiaries to compute their 2002 required distribution using either the final regulations, the 2001 proposed regulations, or the 1987 proposed regulations. Clients will need advice regarding which method is the most favorable for them. The final regulations also require that (for 2003 and later years) all beneficiaries of pre-2002 decedents go back to the date of death and redetermine who is the "designated beneficiary" and what is the "applicable distribution period" using the new rules. Clients will need help with that process.

Previous Year's Distribution. Other aspects of a pre-owned IRA must be considered. This client's father died in 2001, so I started with a discussion of how to calculate the 2002 required distribution for the beneficiary (the client). But what about last year's required distribution? If the father was 75 years old when he died, he was already past the age of 70½, the trigger for required IRA withdrawals. What happens if he had not taken his 2001 distribution before he died on October 31? The beneficiary must take that distribution before the end of the year. Most people think that the father's 2001 distribution (the one that he had not yet taken) should go to the father's estate, but this assumption is incorrect. The beneficiary (the client) owns the IRA the minute the father dies, so the estate does not have any right to the 2001 distribution.

If the father had planned to wait until December 31 to take his required distribution for 2001 and then died on December 30, the beneficiaries have just one day to take their distribution for 2001, which is one of the many reasons I advise clients to take their distributions early in the year. The deceased can leave the beneficiaries in a tough position if he or she dies late in the year without taking the annual distribution. If the deceased dies on December 30, the beneficiaries of the IRA are not immediately going to find out that they are beneficiaries, much less that they are supposed to take that year's required distribution in the last remaining day of the year. As a result, the beneficiaries almost always take the distribution late (after year-end) and have to file with the IRS to ask for a waiver of the penalty. The penalty for not taking a distribution that should have been taken is 50 percent. Although the IRS will probably cancel the penalty under those circumstances, no investment advisor wants to leave the door open for their clients to face a penalty. My advice, therefore, is to take the required distribution early in the year.

Potential Problems. Throughout the preceding section I assumed that when the client appears in the investment advisor's office that she has not yet withdrawn any (or all) of the assets in the IRA, that whatever kind of retirement plan she inherited allows the life expectancy payout method, and that the beneficiary qualifies for the life expectancy payout method. Now I will address what to do if these assumptions are inaccurate.

■ *Cash out.* Suppose the beneficiary cashed out the $1 million inherited IRA *before* visiting her advisor to talk about planning, and the proceeds had already been deposited in her checking account. The problem is that a beneficiary (in general) cannot roll over a distribution from an inherited retirement plan. The exception is for a spouse. If a surviving spouse inherits a retirement plan and cashes it out, he or she is not taxed on the proceeds as long as they are rolled over into another IRA of the same type that was inherited (traditional or Roth) within 60 days. So, if the client's husband dies and leaves her a retirement plan, she can roll the proceeds of the inherited retirement plan over tax free into her own IRA or even into her own employer's retirement plan if her employer's plan permits it. But that is the end of the good news about tax-free rollovers. Children cannot roll over an inherited retirement plan of any type.

■ *Account transfer.* What if the client tried to handle the IRA properly and the financial institution she was dealing with distributed the assets in error? That is, suppose the financial institution transferred the assets in the inherited IRA to an IRA in the client's name because it erroneously believed that such a transfer was allowed under the regulations. The financial institution changed the name of the owner of the inherited IRA from John Jones, the deceased, to Mary Jones, the daughter and heir, which is a no no. This action is not only a distribution but also an illegal rollover contribution to the daughter's IRA. Thus, the daughter will not only have to pay income tax on the distribution, but because she has performed an illegal rollover, she will also have to pay a penalty for an excess IRA contribution. The penalty is only 6 percent, which is a bargain. But transferring the deceased's IRA directly to the name of the beneficiary or to the beneficiary's already established IRA is the wrong way to handle the distribution. And once it is done, it cannot be undone.

The right way to handle the IRA distribution is as follows. The financial institution changes the title on the inherited IRA from "John Jones IRA" to "John Jones Deceased IRA for the Benefit of Mary Jones as Beneficiary." In other words, the father's name stays on the IRA, which makes all the difference. This IRA is not Mary's IRA; it is still her father's IRA. It is an inherited IRA, and as long it is clearly stated that it is an inherited IRA, everything is in good shape. There has been no distribution, which makes the IRS happy, and daughter Mary can start taking the annual minimum required distributions and enjoying the tax-deferred buildup in the meantime.

Financial firms are slowly but surely waking up to the fact that they need to have two separate account agreements for IRAs. One type of agreement should be for "normal" IRAs to which people are making current contributions or those to which rollovers are allowed. The second type of agreement should be for inherited IRAs because they have slightly different provisions.

For example, Mary Jones has inherited an IRA. It is like a normal IRA in the sense that she owns the account and controls the investments and the distributions. But unlike a normal IRA, she cannot make annual contributions to it, nor can she roll over her company's retirement plan into it when she leaves her employer. Because it is an inherited IRA, she has to take distributions from it every year, unlike her own normal IRA from which she does not have to take any distributions until she reaches age 70½. Some of the financial institutions I work with have one account form for regular IRAs (e.g., on white paper) and another form for inherited IRAs (e.g., on pink paper) to prevent confusion.

■ *Lack of life expectancy payout.* One of the biggest problems facing beneficiaries of inherited retirement plans is the fact that many retirement plans do not permit the life expectancy payout. The life expectancy payout is a fabulous tax benefit for people who inherit a retirement plan because they can enjoy tax deferral for their entire lifetime. Why would a retirement plan not offer that option?

Fortunately, most IRAs permit the life expectancy payout, but most company retirement plans take the opposite position. Most 401(k) plans, money purchase plans, profit-sharing plans, and stock bonus plans offer only a lump-sum distribution. This practice happens across the board—whether it is the biggest company in the world or a very small company. So, even though the IRS says the employer can pay the retirement plan money out to the beneficiary over his or her life expectancy, most employers choose otherwise. Employers typically are not in the money management business and do not want to manage money for the employees' children, grandchildren, and so on. Thus, the employer writes the plan so that the only option available to the beneficiary is a lump-sum payment of the benefit. The trouble is, as I said before, a child cannot do a tax-free rollover of the inherited plan to a plan in his or her name (although a spouse can). The child has to take the plan benefit and pay income tax on it. Later in this presentation I will look at charitable giving as one solution to this tremendous problem, but for now (assuming such a charitable arrangement was not made before the employee died) no solution exists.

Although the law is the same for all retirement plans, in reality, the kind of retirement plan a client inherits makes a big difference in the actual financial benefit accruing to the heir. If the client inherited an IRA, the client should be able to use the life expectancy payout to extend the length of time the assets can stay invested in the tax-deferred account, thus maximizing the value of the inherited assets. If the client inherited a 401(k) plan, however, the life expectancy payout option will probably be foreclosed to the client and the lump-sum payout will be taxed immediately, thus leaving a much reduced asset value available for reinvestment.

■ *Beneficiary designation form.* Another problem the advisor might encounter (one that he or she cannot do anything about) in trying to set up the life expectancy payout stems from the beneficiary designation form for the IRA. Continuing with the example in this section, the client is Mary Jones, the daughter of the deceased, John Jones. If the IRA beneficiary designation form says, "I name as my primary beneficiary, my daughter, Mary Jones" everything is fine. She is the beneficiary, and she is entitled to use the life expectancy payout method. But suppose the beneficiary form is blank. In such a case, the advisor must look to the plan documents to determine the disposition of the plan assets. The advisor must contact the IRA provider and request a copy of the account agreement for the IRA, which is not always easy to get. The IRA agreement states what happens to death benefits if a beneficiary is not named, and 99 percent of the time, the default provision is to pay the IRA money to the deceased's estate.

Even though the beneficiary form was not completed, the deceased's will left everything to Mary Jones, his daughter. She is still the beneficiary of the IRA, right? She is entitled to the life expectancy payout method, right? Unfortunately, the IRS says no. The IRS says that in order to benefit from the life expectancy payout method, the beneficiary has to be an individual because only individuals have a life expectancy. An estate, which is not an individual, does not have a life expectancy. Therefore, if the father's benefits are payable to his estate, the estate is not entitled to the life expectancy payout method, and basically, a much faster distribution will be required and taxes will have to be paid much sooner than if the life expectancy payout had been allowed.

Further complexity is added when the IRS's stance on trusts versus estates is considered. When a trust is named as a beneficiary of an IRA, the IRS will look through the trust and treat the individual trust beneficiaries as though they had been named directly as beneficiaries of the IRA as long as certain rules are followed. Thus, an advisor can use the minimum distribution rules and life expectancy payout for trust beneficiaries who are also IRA beneficiaries. Why will the IRS not look through the estate to the beneficiaries of the estate (in this case Mary Jones) and allow the beneficiaries to use the minimum distribution rules? Why does the IRS have a look-through rule for trusts and not for estates? No one knows why.

Effectively the IRS is saying that if the father names his daughter as the beneficiary of his IRA, using her life expectancy, she can withdraw the assets gradually under the minimum distribution rules. If he creates a trust for his daughter and the trust is the beneficiary of his IRA, the trust is eligible to withdraw the assets under the minimum distribution rules using her life expectancy to compute the payouts. But if he names his estate as beneficiary of his IRA (or does not name a beneficiary of the IRA at all) and she is the only beneficiary of his estate, she is not eligible to withdraw the assets using the life expectancy method.

Consequently, advisors need to make sure their clients (assuming they are still alive) fill out their beneficiary designation forms and name human beneficiaries. If a client dies without filling out the beneficiary form and the retirement plan flows into the estate, the beneficiary of the estate probably will not be allowed to take the life expectancy payout. The moral of the story is clear for advisors: Planning is crucial. A retirement plan can be worth a lot of money to heirs if the client names the "right" beneficiary (i.e., if the money does not end up in the estate). But if the client does not name the right beneficiary, the plan could undergo a serious meltdown after the client dies.

■ *Separate accounts.* Until this point I have been using the example that Mary Jones inherited an IRA from her father. But what if three siblings (Mary, Suzie, and Johnny) inherited this account? All three children agree to use the life expectancy payout method, but whose life expectancy should be used? The IRS says that the group has to use the oldest beneficiary's life expectancy, but an exception does exist: If the benefit is divided into separate accounts, one for each of the beneficiaries, then each beneficiary can use his or her own life expectancy.

Particularly if the beneficiaries' age gap is large, it is best to set up separate accounts so each beneficiary can use his or her own life expectancy to calculate required distributions. If Mary is 40 years old, Suzie is 35 years old, and Johnny is 30 years old, Johnny will get 10 extra years of deferral if his account is considered to be separate from Mary's. This separation can be accomplished by either physically having separate accounts for the beneficiaries after death or by having an account agreement that states the account will be treated as separate accounts within the meaning of the regulation.

The concept is that the one IRA is payable to three different people. Even though it is a single IRA, it is actually treated as three separate accounts for bookkeeping purposes, which requires that the siblings account for their shares of the IRA separately and calculate the distributions separately.

The most common way multiple beneficiaries handle the situation is to physically divide the inherited account into separate inherited IRAs. Under the new IRS rules put in place in April 2002, Mary, Suzie, and Johnny have until the end of the year after the year their father died to accomplish that separation. So, if their father died in 2001, naming Mary, Suzie, and Johnny as equal beneficiaries of his IRA, Mary, Suzie, and Johnny must physically divide up that account sometime before the end of 2002. In such a case, the IRA provider would put one-third of the account originally titled "Father, John Jones" into a new account titled "John Jones Deceased Account for the Benefit of Mary Jones as Beneficiary," another one-third of the account into a new account titled "John Jones Deceased for the Benefit of Suzie Jones as Beneficiary," and the final one-third into an account titled "John Jones Deceased for the Benefit of Johnny Jones as Beneficiary." Most beneficiaries prefer to physically divide the account, irrespective of the life expectancy payout issue, simply because doing so allows the greatest flexibility in meeting the individual investment objectives of the beneficiaries.

Under the final regulations issued April 2002, the participant's designated beneficiary for minimum distribution purposes is determined generally as of the date of death but can be modified (via disclaimers and distributions) up until September 30 of the year after death; and "separate accounts" must be established by December 31 of the year after the death of the deceased.

When I counsel a client on estate planning, I suggest that the client clearly state the beneficiary or beneficiaries on the beneficiary designation form for the retirement plan and how the account should be handled upon death. Suppose I have a client who wants to name her three children as beneficiaries. I state on the beneficiary designation form that she is naming her three children as equal beneficiaries and that each child's share will be a separate account within the meaning of the proposed regulation. By setting up the beneficiary designation form in this manner, the accounts are automatically separated on the client's date of death. Granted, under the current rules, beneficiaries have a whole year after the year of death to make these changes, but deadlines are often missed. Explicitly stating the intended separation of accounts on the beneficiary designation form should be done as part of the planning process so that no action in this regard is required by the beneficiaries after the death of the deceased.

■ *IRA provider.* The final problem that can arise in assuring that the beneficiary is able to meet the eligibility requirements for the minimum distribution rules and the life expectancy payout is that the plan administrator or IRA provider can be uncooperative. Suppose I state on the beneficiary designation form for my client that my client's IRA is to be divided into separate accounts for the beneficiaries as of the client's date of death. I send that form to the IRA provider, and the provider returns it saying I have to use the provider's printed form. Suppose that the provider's printed form has a 1-inch space for naming the beneficiary. I can put anything I want in that space, but I cannot add whole paragraphs about separate accounts and the like because they would not fit in the 1-inch space. Thus, a good planning opportunity can be thwarted by an uncooperative IRA provider.

Advising clients who find themselves in such a predicament is difficult. Clients tend to be happy with their investment advisors, so I have a hard time convincing them to use a different investment advisor or IRA provider if their current one is not estate-plan friendly. A large number of wealthy individuals have to take specific steps in their estate planning, such as preparing their beneficiary designation forms, if the planning is to achieve its goal, but I often hear from investment advisors and financial firms that they cannot handle customized beneficiary designation forms. Even though a retirement plan may be a client's largest asset and has a major impact on the client's family financially, many investment advisors and financial firms do not seem to care about the estate-planning needs of their wealthy clients; they just want to manage money. My hope is that more firms will realize the attractiveness of being estate-plan friendly in their IRA administration policies and will welcome customized beneficiary forms.

Plan-to-Plan Transfers. Suppose you are running an investment advisory firm and someone who has just inherited a $1 million IRA walks in the door and asks you to manage it. The only problem is that this IRA is held at a different investment management firm (Mutual Fund B). You want to get those assets over to your firm so you can manage them, but you have a moment of panic. You remember that I said a beneficiary who inherited an IRA could not do a tax-free rollover. So, how can you get that $1 million IRA from Mutual Fund B to your firm? The answer is that even though a beneficiary cannot do a rollover, you can do a custodian-to-custodian transfer tax free. Such a transfer is perfectly legal and is not a rollover. It does not cause a taxable distribution. It is a nonevent.

Mutual Fund B does not give a check to the beneficiary to take to your investment firm to be deposited. That action would be a rollover. Instead, Mutual Fund B sends the assets directly to this newly opened "inherited IRA" at your firm. That action, also called a plan-to-plan transfer, is perfectly fine. The average layperson may have a little difficulty seeing the difference between those two transactions, but to the IRS, they are totally different.

When doing a plan-to-plan transfer of this inherited IRA, the first step is to open the new inherited IRA at your investment advisory firm. Not long ago, this step would have been a problem. The client who inherited the IRA would have gone to your firm and said, "I want to open an IRA for my mother." Your firm would have said, "Fine, have her come in and sign the papers." The client would then have had to say, "She died four months ago. I am trying to open an inherited IRA in the name of my mother who is deceased." This situation would have caused your firm's computer to explode. IRA providers just could not see how someone could open an IRA in the name of a dead person. But the IRS issued several private letter rulings saying that opening such an inherited IRA is perfectly fine. Now, most firms have no problem opening an inherited IRA in the name of the deceased before the IRA is funded by using a transfer from the already established inherited IRA. And remember, the inherited IRA is not going to be opened in the name of the beneficiary alone; it is going to be opened in the name of the deceased, John Jones, for the benefit of Mary Jones.

The next step is getting the money from Mutual Fund B, which, again, is less of a problem than it was a while ago. Financial firms are realizing that in order to attract new accounts, they have to be flexible. That is, they have to be as easy to deal with in setting up newly inherited IRAs as they are when a beneficiary wants to transfer the IRA to a different provider. Occasionally, a firm is still uncooperative, but that attitude is fading and is not encountered frequently.

I mentioned earlier that a beneficiary who inherited a 401(k) plan cannot (in most cases) use the life expectancy payout method but, rather, must take the lump-sum payment. The clever individual might wonder, however, whether the beneficiary cannot simply transfer the money from the inherited 401(k) plan to an inherited IRA and use the life expectancy payout method from the inherited IRA. The answer is that the beneficiary cannot. The IRS's rule is that a transfer from a qualified plan, such as a 401(k) plan, to an IRA is treated as a taxable rollover, even if it is made in a plan-to-plan transfer. Congress has said that children who inherit qualified retirement plans should be able to take distributions over their life expectancy, and by hanging on to this no-transfer rule, Congress is precluding such individuals from taking advantage of the life expectancy payout method that is theoretically available.

The moral of the story is, if a client is in a retirement plan that does not permit a life expectancy payout and that life expectancy payout is important to the client's estate plan, then the client might want to consider rolling the assets out of that plan and into an IRA that would give the beneficiaries better options. The problem is that in some cases, the client cannot (or should not) make such a change. In most cases, employees cannot take the money out of the plan until they terminate employment, and people generally are not going terminate their employment simply to improve their estate plan. Furthermore, if the client's spouse is the beneficiary of the plan, the spouse can do a rollover, so the lump-sum distribution is not a problem. It is true that if the client's spouse does not survive the client, then the children are the beneficiaries and do not have the rollover option. In such a case, the client may want to take out a "second-to-die" life insurance policy that will pay off when the surviving spouse dies, thus providing sufficient funds to compensate for the loss of the income-tax deferral option, or the client may simply be willing to take the chance that his or her children will have to take a lump sum distribution and pay the tax.

For probably 85 percent of the cases, rolling over assets from a qualified plan that does not provide the life expectancy payout method to an IRA is preferable. The estate plan, however, is not the only consideration when contemplating whether an IRA rollover is appropriate. In some instances, taking the lump-sum distribution and paying the income taxes on it is a good idea. For example, taking the lump sum is a good idea when the client holds in the plan a large amount of company stock that qualifies for favorable tax treatment as appreciated employer securities.[2] Or the client may qualify for 10-year averaging, which significantly lowers the applicable tax rate on the distribution, if the client was born before 1936, again making the lump-sum option attractive.

Another consideration before the rollover decision is made is creditor protection. Some clients are concerned about asset protection issues, and in some states, money is better protected from creditors if it is in a company plan rather than an IRA. Another factor in the rollover decision might be state income taxes. Some states tax an IRA differently from a qualified pension distribution. So, although estate planning is an important factor in the rollover decision, it is not the only factor.

Tax Concerns. The following tax concerns must also be taken into account when working with pre-owned IRAs: double taxation and accelerated distributions.

Double taxation. Both estate taxes and income taxes are levied on retirement benefits. Suppose the estate tax rate is 50 percent and the beneficiary of the estate is in the top income-tax bracket—approximately 40 percent. One might think for a $1 million IRA that the estate pays a 50 percent estate tax and then the beneficiary pays a 40 percent income tax, which adds up to taxation of 90 percent. Actually, the situation is not quite as bad as that. If a beneficiary inherits a retirement plan that was subject to estate tax, the beneficiary, in effect, gets a deduction on his or her income-tax return for the estate tax that was paid on that asset. In other words, theoretically, the beneficiary will pay income tax on $500,000 of the $1 million IRA (the balance left after the estate pays the 50 percent estate tax). So, the beneficiary does not pay 40 percent income tax on the whole IRA but only on the half that is left after the estate tax is paid. Thus, the total tax bill is not 90 percent (50 percent plus 40 percent), but 70 percent (50 percent plus 20 percent).

This tax still sounds high, but keep in mind that all assets are subject to double taxation. Whether income is derived from compensation or from investments, income tax (as high as 38.6 percent) must be paid on every dollar of income. The accumulated after-tax income left in the estate at death is then taxed at a 50 percent rate if the estate is larger than the exemption amount.[3] So, retirement plans are no worse than other assets in terms of the tax burden. The benefit of the retirement plan location is that the nearly 40 percent income tax payment is deferred, but it is not eliminated. And all things being equal, the individual is better off paying the tax later by deferring it through the retirement plan.

---

[2] Under some circumstances, the taxation of net unrealized appreciation in stock of the sponsoring employer distributed from the employer's qualified retirement plan can be deferred until the employer stock is sold. Upon the later sale of that stock, the net unrealized appreciation is taxed as a long-term capital gain. There is no 10 percent penalty tax on the net unrealized appreciation (either when distributed or sold) or on dividends paid on the employer stock, even if the participant is under age 59½.

[3] In 2002 and 2003, the exemption amount is $1 million; in 2004, the exemption amount increases to $1.5 million; and by 2009, the exemption amount increases to $3.5 million. Under current tax law, in 2010, the estate tax is to be repealed.

If the advisor is dealing with a *fait accompli*—the beneficiaries inherited the retirement plan and immediately cashed it out—the advisor should remind them to take the deduction for the estate taxes that they paid. Furthermore, the advisor should make sure the beneficiaries know that the deduction goes to the person who inherited the plan, not to the person who paid the estate tax. Imagine a situation in which a father dies. He leaves all his probate assets to his son, who is to pay all the estate taxes out of his share of his father's estate. The father leaves his IRA to his daughter, and because in his estate plan the son will pay the entire estate tax bill, she does not have to pay any estate taxes. So, even though she did not pay the estate taxes, she still gets the income-tax deduction for the estate taxes—taxes that her brother paid on the IRA she inherited.

■ *Accelerated distributions.* Is taking a distribution from a retirement plan before death rather than after death, sooner rather than later, ever a good idea? Consider the following scenario: Assume a client wants to take a premature distribution, pay ordinary income tax on it, and pay bills with the remaining proceeds. (In this case, if the client is under age 59½, an early withdrawal penalty of 10 percent is generally applicable.) Ideally, the client would take out a home mortgage (with tax-deductible interest) or find another source of income to pay the bills rather than depleting his or her retirement plan with taxable distributions, but sometimes the client has no other option. Or perhaps the client wants to take a distribution of appreciated employer stock; the distribution is immediately taxable but only to the extent of the original value of the stock when it was placed in the employee's retirement account. The rest of the stock's value is called "net unrealized appreciation" (NUA) of employer stock, which is not subject to ordinary income tax at withdrawal but is subject to a 20 percent capital gains tax when the stock is sold. (In this case, if the client is under 59½, the 10 percent early withdrawal penalty applies only to the portion of the distribution that is taxed when distributed; it does not apply to the "net unrealized appreciation" portion of the stock, even when the stock is sold.) If the purpose of the early withdrawal is to invest in a potentially appreciating asset, an immediate income tax is levied on the distribution, but the advantage that counterbalances the immediate taxation is that the investment made with the distribution, if held until the client's death, will get a step-up in basis as it passes from the client's estate to the estate's beneficiary. Thus, neither the client nor the beneficiary will have to pay capital gains tax on the appreciated asset that originated with the retirement plan distribution.

Regardless of when a distribution is made from a retirement plan, the distribution will always be subject to income tax. The assets in the plan, however, do not get a step-up in basis in the client's estate. In any event, double taxation is not avoided by early withdrawals. In fact, withdrawing the money from the plan sooner than is required merely accelerates one part of the double tax—the income tax; it in no way eliminates the double tax. And the benefits of paying income tax sooner rather than later and of a step-up in basis must be weighed carefully.

Now consider this scenario: Father is on his deathbed. He has $1 million in a 401(k) plan that does not offer the option of the life expectancy payout for beneficiaries. His estate is large enough to be subject to estate taxes, and each of his children (who are also his beneficiaries) is in a high income-tax bracket. The children would benefit if the father cashes out the plan and pays the income taxes while he is still alive; the income-tax bill on the plan will reduce the size of his estate, and hence the estate tax will be smaller. The other alternative is, of course, not to cash out the plan before father dies, pay the estate tax on the whole estate (including the funds that could have gone to pay the income tax on the premature distribution of the plan), and have each child pay his or her respective income tax bill on his or her portion of the inherited plan.

Theoretically, paying 40 percent income tax first and then 50 percent estate tax on the remaining balance should be the same as paying 50 percent estate tax first and then 40 percent income tax on the remaining balance. But reality does not match theory in this situation because the beneficiaries' income-tax deduction for estate taxes is not perfect for two reasons. First of all, the beneficiary does not get an income-tax deduction for state inheritance taxes or estate taxes. So, if the father cashes out the plan before dying, both the federal income tax and state income tax are out of his estate tax base for estate tax purposes. If he dies before cashing out the plan, the children will have to pay federal and state estate taxes on the plan benefit, but they can only deduct the federal estate tax on their income-tax returns. Second, the income-tax deduction is an itemized deduction that is subject to a reduction of 3 percent of excess deductions for taxpayers with more than $130,000 of income. So, high-income taxpayers are probably not going to get the full benefit of the income-tax deduction for estate taxes.

The result is an arbitrage situation. If the advisor knows that the money will be cashed out shortly after death and that the client is about to die, the advisor serves the beneficiaries better by having the client cash out the plan shortly before death rather than having the beneficiaries cash it out shortly after death. The problem is that no advisor knows exactly when someone is going to die (or what constitutes shortly before death). Additionally, the advisor does not always know if the beneficiaries are going to cash the plan out right away, which creates a complicated planning situation. Therefore, there is no pat answer to whether a client should take an accelerated distribution from a retirement plan.

Death of the Beneficiary. So far I have concentrated on a beneficiary's concerns with an inherited, pre-owned retirement plan. But what happens when the beneficiary dies? Continuing with the example I gave earlier, suppose that Mary Jones begins to take the required minimum distributions from her inherited IRA over the 44.6 years specified as her life expectancy in the IRS's life expectancy tables. What happens if she dies in Year 30? Who gets the money from the IRA, and how fast does it have to come out after Mary dies?

The second question (concerning how fast the money needs to come out) is easier to answer than the first question because her death has no effect on the required distributions from that account. Her death in Year 30 of a 44.6-year payout does not accelerate the distributions. Her death does not stretch the payments out any further; it is a totally neutral event. The payout period is still the 44.6 years that was established when she inherited the account.

The tougher question is the first one (concerning who gets the money). The answer depends on the IRA agreement and her estate plan. For example, some IRA providers (the ones I call the enlightened, estate-plan friendly IRA providers) say that Mary Jones, who inherited this IRA, can name her own beneficiary for it, which the IRS says is fine. The IRA does not have to go through probate, and Mary can, on her beneficiary designation form, state that if she dies before she receives all of the distributions, the remaining payments should go to her spouse or her children—whomever she wants. So, when Mary dies, the IRA provider transfers the account to whomever Mary has designated as her beneficiary. Thus, the enlightened IRA providers are permitting and encouraging beneficiaries to name successor beneficiaries so that they can avoid probate. The IRS specifically says in its regulations that IRA providers can allow beneficiaries to name successor beneficiaries; the IRS has no problem with it, so theoretically, the IRA provider should have no problem with it either.

Death Pre-January 2001. In January 2001, favorable new regulations on how to determine post-death required distributions were instituted by the IRS. Everyone can use the new rules, regardless of date of death. In most cases, that change is favorable for the beneficiary. For example, suppose a daughter inherited an IRA from her father, who died in the 1990s. The new rules enable her to use her own life expectancy for the payments she has not yet received; in many cases, the old rules would have had her using a much faster payout period.

Why would the IRS be so incredibly kind hearted and generous as to allow beneficiaries to switch over to the new rules even if the person they inherited the IRA from died before these rules came into effect? The answer is that if the IRS kept the old set of rules for everyone who died before January 2001 and then added the new rules for everyone dying after January 2001, it would have to keep both sets of rules alive forever. And keeping both sets of rules would also mean that IRA administrators would have to maintain the capability to calculate distributions under two different methods. So, everybody has to switch to the new minimum distribution calculation rules starting in 2003. The switch is optional for 2002. For most people, the switch to the new rules produces a favorable result.

Charitable Strategies

Charitable giving can solve some of the problems with retirement benefits that I mentioned earlier. The main attraction of charitable giving is that it addresses the issue of double taxation. I typically try to encourage my clients to think of their retirement plans as a partnership with the IRS, whereby the IRS has a "mortgage" on their retirement plans. So, a client with a $1 million IRA must remember that the IRS has a mortgage on that IRA of 40 percent, representing the income taxes that have not yet been paid. For each dollar the client takes out of the plan, the client has to pay off 40 cents of the mortgage that the IRS owns. By getting my clients to think of their retirement plans in this way, I can work with them to constructively plan how to reduce the impact of the mortgage, get the money out at a lower rate, or buy off the mortgage cheaply.

Throughout this presentation I have been mostly talking about the strategy of deferring the payment of the income tax by naming a child or grandchild as a beneficiary. With charitable giving, I am talking about a different strategy—getting rid of the mortgage altogether. Gifts to charity are estate tax free and income tax free. In the simplest example, the client dies, leaves the IRA to charity, and the IRS gets nothing. The planning implication is that for the client who is charitably inclined, the advisor should try very hard to use retirement assets for charitable gifts. Thus, the easiest way to carry out this plan is if the client says, "I want to leave $1 million to my favorite art museum," and the client has a $1 million IRA to dedicate toward carrying out that intent. In this case, the advisor should have the client name the art museum as the beneficiary of the IRA. Unfortunately, clients never seem to want to handle the situation that way. They want to leave the charity a formula amount, or they want to leave some to charity and some to the family. In this situation, the advisor needs to make sure that the gift to charity does not interfere with the family members being able to use the life expectancy payout method.

The charitable remainder trust (CRT) provides a solution for three estate planning problems. The CRT is the workhorse of charitable giving. With a CRT, a human beneficiary receives an income for his or her life (or for a term of up to 20 years). The human beneficiary's income from the trust can be a fixed dollar amount, such as $50,000 a year, called an annuity, or a fixed percentage amount, such as 5 percent of the value of the trust every year. When the life income is a fixed dollar amount, the CRT is called a charitable remainder annuity trust (CRAT), and when the life income is a fixed percentage amount, the CRT is called a charitable remainder unit trust (CRUT). I will focus on the CRUT, which is the more commonly used vehicle. The concept is that the client leaves the $1 million IRA to a CRUT. The trust then pays the surviving spouse, say, 5 percent of the trust value every single year, whether the spouse needs it or not, and on the spouse's death, the trust pays all the money that is left in the trust to the client's favorite charity. Assuming a 5 percent annual rate of return on the investments in the trust, theoretically, the entire $1 million will get passed on to the charity.

The advantage of this strategy is that the deceased can accomplish his or her charitable goals while also financially providing for a spouse or other heirs and escape income taxation on the IRA's assets that flow into the CRUT. One drawback is that the spouse can only get the fixed percentage (in this example, 5 percent) of income annually. If the spouse needs more money for medical expenses, the money cannot come from the trust. So, a CRUT is not an estate-planning vehicle for all the assets in a client's estate, but in certain cases, it is useful.

The following example shows how useful a CRUT can be. One of my clients had a substantial retirement benefit payable from several plans. The client wanted to provide for some of his adult family members of varying ages. This client also had a charitable intent for the ultimate disposition of these assets. One option would have been to set up the retirement plans to be payable to a trust and to give the trustee the discretion to help these adult family members. The trustee, however, would have had to withdraw all of the retirement plan benefits over the life expectancy of the oldest member of this family group, who happened to be close to 80—not a very long life expectancy. Consequently, the distributions would have occurred rapidly, thereby accelerating the income-tax bill. By putting the retirement plans into a CRUT, the CRUT was able to pay income generated by the entire principal of the retirement plans (rather than just income generated by the amount remaining after paying income tax on the retirement plans) to these family members, and because the percentage is fixed, the family members cannot bother the trustee every time they want to increase their expenditures. The client avoided the high trust income-tax rates that normally apply to retirement benefits payable to a trust because a CRUT is an income-tax-exempt vehicle. And the CRUT also allowed the client to make a sizable charitable contribution. Furthermore, the client avoided the problem of having a trustee collect minimum distributions from several different plans. The plans were all put into one CRUT, and at the date of death, the individual plans were obliterated, which solves a practical estate-planning problem.

Charitable giving can also solve one of the biggest problems with retirement plans—when the plan pays only a lump-sum distribution death benefit. I mentioned earlier that this problem cannot be avoided because the individual has no power to alter the terms of his or her employer's qualified retirement plan. The following example shows how I got around this problem for one client, a business executive in her early 60s with no plans to retire for several years. Normally, a charitable-giving device only works for someone with a charitable intent. But in this case, the client made a "profit" with charitable giving. The client had accumulated a huge amount in a profit-sharing plan. She wanted her adult children to be the beneficiaries. The only form of distribution from the plan was a lump sum. She could roll the plan over to an IRA but only after she retired because the plan would not distribute any funds until she retired. At the time she came to me, she did not want to retire for several more years.

If she had directed the plan to pay a lump sum to her two children (who were in the highest tax bracket), taxes would have eaten up most of the money. Instead, we decided to make the plan payable to a CRUT with a life interest for the two children who were in their 40s, and on the death of the surviving child, the balance of the CRUT would go to her favorite charity. The numbers showed that if her two children lived to their probable life expectancy, the income they would get from the CRUT over their lifetimes, plus the accumulated value of the estate tax deduction for this charitable gift, would be worth more dollars to them than if they had been named directly as beneficiaries of the retirement plan. If they were named directly as beneficiaries, they would have had to take one lump-sum distribution and would have received no charitable deduction on the estate tax return. Thus, their net inheritance would have been less than if they had been life beneficiaries of a CRUT. In this case, the client profited from charitable giving. Even though this client was not charitably inclined, she opted for the CRUT because it worked in her favor.

Conclusion

Retirement benefits are becoming an increasingly significant asset in an individual's portfolio because of changes in the laws that allow employees to save more money in their plans and to keep the money in their plans longer. And because of changing demographics of the population, more people are nearing retirement every year, thus increasing the demand for the services of investment advisors. Not only are retirement plans becoming increasingly important to the employee, they are also becoming increasingly important to the employee's beneficiaries. With careful planning, an advisor can help a client's beneficiaries get the most out of their inherited retirement plans or IRAs. Taking advantage of the life expectancy payout method, plan-to-plan transfers, and charitable strategies are a few of the ways an advisor can help beneficiaries maximize their benefits.

Succession Planning for a First-Generation Family Business

Fredda Herz Brown
Founder, Managing Partner, and Senior Consultant
The Metropolitan Group, LLC
Tenafly, New Jersey

> Proper succession planning for the transfer of a family business between the first and second generations can set the stage for the future success of the business. To illustrate the complexities of ownership, business, and family issues, a case study is presented along with suggestions on how to avoid some of the most common pitfalls in family business succession planning.

Many people expect family businesses to be disasters, and family businesses indeed frequently fail. I view family businesses in a completely different way, however. I think of them as tremendous opportunities to teach young people about the world of business and the world in general. And the more the family business is seen as an opportunity, the less likely the family will go from poor to rich to poor in three generations.

Families Who Share Assets

Not long ago, the family business and wealth management were sequential functions. The family office—one entity combining investment management, family business operations, tax compliance, intergenerational wealth transfer planning, and many other functions—did not get created until the family business was sold and a large pot of wealth needed to be managed. But in the past 10 years, a significant change has taken place. More families are forming what I call "enterprises." Families no longer choose to sell the extant family business and then move on to a "retirement" phase to enjoy their wealth; rather, I see families operating a variety of business ventures through multiple generations, which makes dealing with a family business much more interesting and complex than in the past.

In addition to the fact that families grow more complex over time, the family enterprise becomes more complex. This trend became apparent to me at a seminar I gave to wealthy families about two years ago. Of the nine people at this seminar, four had recently sold their businesses—businesses that had been passed down to them by their families—and had started new enterprises within a short period of time. Four of the other five people at the seminar were in the process of readying their businesses to be sold and making plans for how they would use their resources from the sale of the business. Only one person had not made any kind of decision about what to do with the family business/enterprise.

A significant challenge for families is staying together as a unit over time. For those of us in the family business field, the focus has always been on keeping families together and creating the necessary "glue." But equally important is providing a way out for those family members who want one. As families grow, they become much more complex; the enterprises they manage become more complicated, and the connection to the person who originally founded the business becomes weaker. So, at the same time we talk about the importance of family meetings and getting family members together to manage the family business and conduct the business of the family, we also need to think about how to create reasonable exit strategies and liquidity for any family members who no longer wish to be part of the business.

A family business creates unique dynamics. How many people have to (or have the opportunity to) deal with their family members (brothers, sisters, etc.) in adulthood in an environment where they make major decisions together? Unless you are part of a family business, you will not typically have that kind of experience. Family members are joined together not only in business decision making but also in protecting the family business by preventing outsiders from viewing the family dynamics. I have a dear friend who has been part of a family business for years. She says that in a family enterprise, the family members close ranks tightly so that outsiders will not be privy to what is going on inside the business. Any exposure of negative family dynamics to the outside world threatens to cast a dark shadow on both the family and the reputation of the family business.

Generational transitions in terms of ownership and management of the family business become more complex over time because of new and departing family members. Not only does the business itself become more intricate, but the family and family relationships also become more intricate. Consider in-laws who enter a family business. Typically when a person gets married, he or she is concerned about how to deal with the new mother-in-law, father-in-law, sister-in-law, and so on. But when a person marries into a family enterprise, that person also has to figure out his or her position vis-à-vis that entity because several ways exist for the new family member to become integrated into the family enterprise.

First-Generation Transition

A first-generation transition of a family business is important because it sets the tone for how every other transition will be handled in that family enterprise. The more thought that is put into the first transition, the less difficult the transition to subsequent generations. For instance, I have just been involved in a lawsuit in which the fourth generation of a family business sued other family members to right perceived wrongs against earlier generations. The origins of the lawsuit could be traced back to previous difficult generational transitions. In this family, the patriarch of the family enterprise brought all seven of his children into the business, even though none of them had a particular interest in the business. Three of the siblings thought they were not treated as well as the other four siblings and passed these feelings on to their children, who heard stories at the dinner table about how their fathers had not been treated fairly by their patriarch a generation earlier. The result was that the children in one branch of the family sued the children in the four other branches to get what they felt their fathers had not gotten in the generation before—fairness and more opportunity in the business. Thus, the original business transition model (or the lack thereof) sets up the dynamic for future transitions, and the fallout from preceding generational transitions becomes manifest in the attitudes of the most current generation.

Family Enterprise System

A model for family enterprises views them as three interlocking circles of relationships, ownership, and the business. When creating a model for a first-generation transition or any generational transition, it is helpful to think in terms of this system of interlocking circles, as shown in **Figure 1**. The "relationship" circle defines the emotional connections between people, from those who are friends to those who are family. In a first-generation family business, all the circles—relationships, business, and ownership—are bound together as one, with all

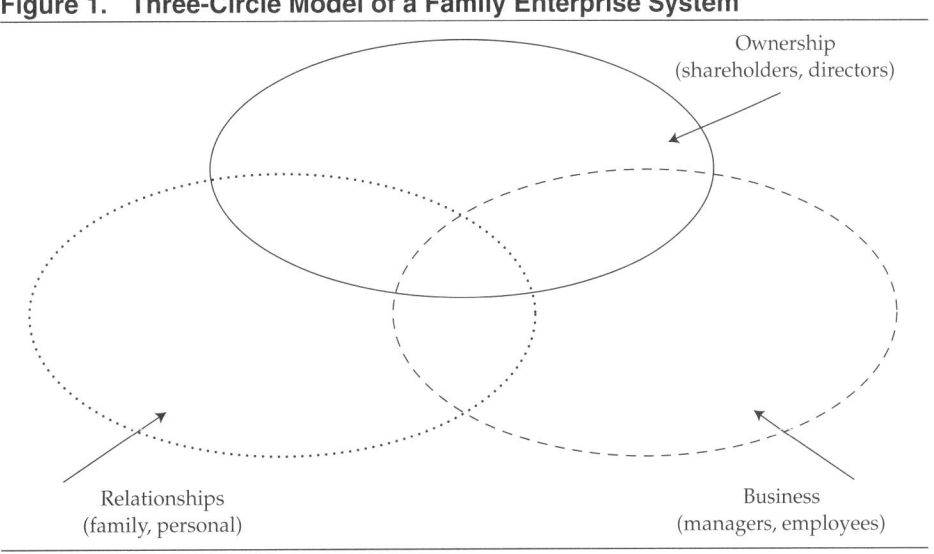

Figure 1. Three-Circle Model of a Family Enterprise System

Ownership (shareholders, directors)

Relationships (family, personal)

Business (managers, employees)

Source: Owner Management Business Institute, 1989.

three functions combined in one person. As time goes on and the business becomes more involved and the family grows in size, the three circles separate but remain interlocked so that the relationship, ownership, and business functions do not necessarily all reside in one person anymore.

What these separate but interlocking circles mean is that when planning for a business transition, the impact any one circle has on the other circles must be considered. For instance, a decision about ownership can affect the family for generations to come. Setting up a grandparental trust in order to establish a transition of the ownership of the family business to the grandchildren without a conversation between the grandparents and the parents of the grandchildren creates a particular kind of family relationship that might not be desirable. Accordingly, whenever working with a family enterprise, a decision's effect on all three circles must be weighed carefully.

A family business has multiple constituent groups, each with its own voice. Each voice differs in terms of what its needs are. At the center of the relationship system is usually the person who founded the family business, and for a first- to second-generation transfer, that person is typically still at the center. This person holds most, if not all, of the capital in the business. But in order to have a successful and adequate transition, that person has to be replaced in some respects in the ownership and business circles. The transition has to be done on a timely basis and according to a well-defined timeline. Often the children who are working in the business ask when they will get ownership of the business, and the parent answers that the ownership of the business will be passed on only when the children prove they can run the business. They go round and round. Without a transition plan, the two generations are often at odds and the business frequently suffers.

One of my first experiences working with a family enterprise involved a father whose three sons worked in the family business. Their raises were based on whether they were married and how many children they had had the year before, not on their performance in the business. This founder's vantage point was totally on the family relationship side and not at all on the business side. One can imagine how such a model plays out by, say, the third generation. The third generation typically has many more family members who have ownership but who are not working in the business. In this type of situation, tensions are high, resulting in a desire to liquidate their ownership interests in the family enterprise for family members who are not involved in the day-to-day operations of the business because of the inappropriate compensation plans paid to the family members involved in the business. These tensions can best be managed by devising family enterprise exit strategies before that type of situation unfolds.

A typical first- to second-generation transition is from owner/manager to owner/manager (from one person to another person) or, more likely, owner/manager to sibling partnerships, in which a number of the children want to enter the family business. The questions then become how the siblings should own and manage the business jointly and what model should be in place for decision making in this business. The more experience young family members have in talking together about family and business issues as they grow up, the more successful they will be at making the first- to second-generation transition in the family enterprise.

Objectifying the Family Business

I see my work with family enterprises as an effort to help families create more-objective business structures. I work with family members to set up structures and decision-making mechanisms so that they can run the enterprise in a way that is reasonable for them—a way that keeps their business from totally overtaking their family life and that keeps their family from totally overtaking their business life. Adopting a specific structure or framework for communicating about important decisions and then making those decisions is an important element that allows the family as a unit to adequately respond to its various constituent concerns. Beyond the actual structures adopted, the family and its advisors must work to develop mechanisms, policies, and agreements to deal with the different processes within the family and the family's business.

I believe that the family business consultant's role is to help the family develop structures that closely match the constituency groups within the family. A good guideline for developing these structures is to consider the structures appropriate to each of the three circles in the relationship system in Figure 1. One such structure in the ownership circle is an outside board of directors—independent directors outside the family. But getting first- and second-generation family members to agree to an outside board of directors is no easy task. It is so important, however, that we have established a small division of our firm to focus solely on developing boards of directors for family enterprises.

Although we find a tremendous amount of resistance to creating an outside board of directors, it is probably the best thing a family could ever do, other than having regular family meetings. The primary advantage of an outside board of directors is the objectivity it provides in the management of the business—a trait that family members often lack. Without such a board, how can family members, who often have conflicting goals, lengthy family histories, and emotional entanglements, reasonably make objective business decisions? One of the best ways to make good decisions is to invite outsiders into the process by asking them to join the board. Families who either want to experiment with or are resistant to the idea of an outside board can develop an advisory board in lieu of a full-fledged operating board.

A necessary structure involving the ownership issue is regular shareholder meetings. Shareholder meetings are distinct from family meetings because not all family members are shareholders; these meetings address issues related to the ownership of stock, voting that stock, and governance. Such meetings are important because they call attention to the fact that certain family members actually have ownership in the family business and others do not.

In the family circle, a structure is needed that encourages and supports the family to meet as a group and talk about family and business issues. To increase the likelihood that the family can maintain and grow the business in the future and accomplish a transition beyond the second generation, family members need to be educated about the family business and how it affects both shareholders and nonshareholders. Thus, having some kind of family forum, meeting, or council, whatever it is called, not only helps educate family members but also gets them talking about how the family can operate as a unit and make important decisions together. Governance of the family enterprise—a broader concept than just the family business entity—is a critical issue.

In the business circle, the organization and running of the business is relatively straightforward. Executive management meetings, partnership and partnering agreements, and relationship contracting are all parts of the business structure that can strengthen and grow the business. A more challenging and complex task, however, is incorporating the family's mission (its reason for keeping the business) into the development of the business.

Another concern involving the business is how to accomplish a graceful, rather than rushed, transition of family business ownership from one owner or group of owners to another owner or group of owners within or outside the family. In my experience, a graceful transition takes about 8 to 10 years, evolves over time, and affects all three circles in a family enterprise system. If ownership is being transferred from one generation to another, an estate plan generally has to be in place and the family must decide how family members can enter and exit the business. Families need a structure for how a family member applies and gets accepted to participate in the business. Oftentimes, children come to the business not to work with one another but to work with their parents, but then they are stuck working with each other. An extremely important part of that transition process is having the children express their dreams and goals and how they want to put them into action in the business. Thus, all three circles—ownership, business, and relationships—need to be aligned at the point of transition to accomplish a graceful transition.

Common Pitfalls in Succession Planning

Unfortunately, family business succession planning is not always done, and even when the process is started, it is typically not given sufficient time or attention. A common stumbling block is an inadequately developed plan or a plan that considers only one aspect of the family business. An important consideration is including the family members, family office staff, and nonfamily business owners—all of whom will be affected by the business succession plan—in the development of the plan. Family businesses are too often the victims of a lack of proper planning and/or poor planning on the part of the founder and owner. Educating family members using the structures of a relationship system—such as family meetings and shareholder meetings—is a good antidote to counteract inadequate business succession planning.

Case Study

As I mentioned earlier, family meetings are a necessary family structure that helps align the interests of family members and aids the operation of the family business. Family meetings encourage the establishment and maintenance of a family culture and the transfer of the family mission to successive generations. The following case study allows for an examination of which family members, family business employees, and family advisors would be meeting and the possible concerns of each person at a meeting defined as a family meeting—in this case, the Chase family meeting.

THE CHASES AND CHASE, INC.

Chase, Inc., is a fairly large land development and real estate holding company begun in 1960 by John Chase with current holdings of $150 million (gross). John still remains the major stockholder of the holding company; his wife, Jenny, owns 25 percent, and each of his two children own 7.5 percent.

The most recent uproar began when, without consultation, John gave 5 percent of his stock to a faithful employee, the CFO of the holding company; John now owns 55 percent of the stock. His children, John, Jr., and Ruth, feel that their father has once again bypassed them in decision making. Both have threatened to leave the business in which they have worked for a long time.

John, Jr., (J.J. as he is called) is a 40-year-old "wonder boy." Although his father started the business when he was 15 years younger than J.J. is now, J.J. has received a fine education in finance and money management and has inherited his father's great sense for land development. During the time he has been V.P. for Land Projects and Investments, the company has grown from $5 million to its current value. J.J. has worked for the company for 15 years and receives a salary of $300,000 a year and has the opportunity to invest directly in real estate investments.

Ruth, his younger sister, is a very talented architect/designer who worked in the company first part time and now full time. She acts as an architect for some of their real estate holdings, cleverly designing new uses for old sites. She has recently developed some properties into very successful office and marketing space without any ownership in these investments. Ruth has worked with her brother and father for 10 years. She gets a salary of $200,000. She feels she should be paid more in line with her brother's salary and has told her father and brother she feels that way. Like her brother, she is married with several children.

Ruth and J.J.'s spouses are not employed by the company but are very concerned about the ongoing time involvement of their spouses with little overall ownership. However, Ruth's spouse is educated as an accountant. He would eventually like to work in the company, but a decision about this has not yet been reached in the family.

Jenny, their mother, does not work in the company now but did once as John's "right-hand woman" doing the books, handling phones, and so on while John searched for and researched properties for development. Her 25 percent of the stock feels like a burden at times, creating a sense of responsibility and obligation for a company she no longer understands. She and John spend a lot of time together at their home in Florida. She would like for him to retire. They have talked about dispersing their assets, including the business, but can't reach a decision. Jenny believes the children would do okay without John in the business, and she is tired of being the "go-between," hearing the complaints from both children about each other and from her husband about the children.

Matt, the CFO, has been with the company for 22 years helping John develop the company and serving as the money manager since the company's inception. He now works closely with the offspring, J.J. and Ruth, but still remembers who takes care of him. Jenny has told John that she thinks he is too attached to Matt and has given him too much power.

Because the children have threatened to resign, John has called a family meeting to hear all "voices" and to develop a succession plan. A professional facilitator was invited to attend. Following is a list of those attending the meeting:

- Founder (John),
- Jenny,
- Ruth,
- J.J.,
- Non family employee (Matt), and
- In-law spouses.

If the Chase family had had in place a regular, established structure of family meetings to discuss the issues of importance to the family as they arose, the nature of the family meeting just described would be altered; in particular, it would not be so fraught with the emotions of the family members in connection with their own agendas and fears. The following discussion examines the likely concerns of each of the members who will be participating in the Chase family meeting.

■ *John's concerns.* John (the founder of the company and the father) could be afraid of losing control of his business. John's ego might also be a concern. The founder of a business sometimes spends more time with the business than with his or her children. The business becomes like a child. A client of mine (one of four sisters) described her father's business as "the fifth daughter at the dinner table." Figuratively speaking, she believed that in her father's eyes, the family business occupied a bigger place at the dinner table than any of the four sisters. Her father was more attached to his "fifth child" than to any of the four daughters. Often, the founder is so involved in the business that his or her ego becomes a problem at family meetings. John may feel threatened by the minority shareholders criticizing his transfer of ownership to Matt, a nonfamily member, regardless of his loyalty and tenure of 22 years. John may feel that the children have no right to criticize him and that the decision was his to make. Or he may feel he had to offer Matt ownership in order to keep him.

The preservation and continuance of the business would certainly be a concern of John. The founder is often uncertain about whether he or she should sell or give the business to the children. The correct decision is a product of the family's culture and its way of interacting. Experience has shown me that children are more appreciative of that which they have to work for or buy themselves.

John might be truly worried about what will happen to his children if they work in the business together. How will they manage their sibling relationships and their business relationships? I have discovered that when siblings work together in the business, they see less of each other outside work because they spend so much time together at work. As a parent, the founder may be concerned about how the business will affect the children's personal relationships.

A final, significant issue from John's point of view is whether enough assets will remain after his estate is settled to still run the business.

■ *Jenny's concerns.* Jenny (the mother) wants her husband to retire, but in the current environment, she has a central position managing the conflicts between her children and her husband. Without the conflicts, she could lose her central position. So, at the same time that a good relationship among family members is desirable, it might also be detrimental in that Jenny could lose her central role as a family mediator.

Jenny could also be worried that she will get drawn back into the business if John passes away—a situation she would not welcome. And finally, Jenny may be upset that Matt was given shares in the company and her children were not. So, Jenny may be walking into the meeting with the desire to make sure that her children get what is rightfully theirs.

■ *J.J.'s and Ruth's concerns.* The children might be worried that their ownership in the company is not commensurate with their contributions to the company. And they might be worried about the issue of compensation once their father retires. Usually, a major transition issue in a family enterprise is how compensation will be decided after the founder leaves (assuming the founder has been making all those decisions).

The larger question, however, is about much more than compensation. It is about what is going to happen in the long term in this business. Is J.J. going to get control and make all the decisions? Or is the business going to be a collective effort? Will one of the children have ownership control and the other have management control? J.J. and Ruth might be surprised, and concerned, about the gift of shares to Matt. Although one might think that they should have seen this gift coming (after all, they would have seen how their father has relied on Matt for the past 22 years), they probably never had any explicit discussions about it with their father. So, even though the children might have known how much their father relies on Matt, they may have expected that some portion of their father's shares would pass to them or that at least they would have a voice in the decision to give shares to Matt.

Furthermore, both J.J. and Ruth might have concerns about Ruth's husband wanting to join the business. When in-laws enter the business, questions arise about who can vote, how they will vote, and how they will fit into the business. And what does it mean for Ruth to have her husband enter the business? Family businesses in the major transition from first generation to second generation need to outline the rules for entry into the enterprise, although these rules can change over time because the decisions made at the first transition may not be appropriate for the second transition.

J.J. and Ruth might also be wondering whether they want to stay in the business. Often, family enterprises do not give children enough opportunities to explore possibilities beyond the family enterprise. If a family member is staying in the family business only because he or she thinks that is the only place where he or she can work, that does not bode well for the business or the family.

The children may also be wondering what will happen to Matt's shares and how he will dispose of them now that he has become an owner. At this point, the family does not have any guidelines about how decisions will be made about the family's legacy—this enterprise. They do not have a charter that talks about what the mission of this family is or what the vision of the family is in terms of keeping the business. Do they want to keep it, and if they are going to keep it, how are they going to run it in the future?

Ruth might be concerned about the fact that J.J. has the opportunity to invest in some of the business's real estate investments but she does not. She may want the same opportunity. For example, one family I work with has four sons, one of whom works in the business along with his wife. Each sibling has an ownership interest in the family's real estate business and gets an equal amount of the real estate investments made, but the son who works in the business and his wife get to invest in an additional 6 percent of every real estate deal. This situation has thrown the family into an uproar. No guidelines have ever been set to deal with this type of situation. Without guidelines, the potential for conflicts to arise is considerable.

■ *Matt's concerns.* Matt might not really want to be at the meeting. He may think that these are decisions that the family needs to make. He probably feels like the bad guy walking into the meeting and worries that everyone will see him as the cause of any problems. He may be thinking of asking for a cash settlement instead of the shares. He may also be thinking that with his 22 years at the company, he can be very helpful to J.J. and Ruth. When a large age difference exists between the first generation and the second generation and the second generation is not yet ready to take over the business, having a person like Matt around is important. He could become a tremendous leader and help the second generation grow into the business, which would be an impetus for John to keep Matt happy.

■ *The in-laws' concerns.* The in-laws might be wondering what they are doing at this meeting because they do not have ownership in the business. But supposedly this is a family meeting, not a business meeting, which is a source of confusion.

Ruth's husband, in particular, might want to know how he can join the business. At this point, he may be feeling somewhat excluded because no guidelines have been established for him to enter the business. He is probably walking into the meeting feeling slightly on the outside and wondering what he needs to do to get on the inside. And the other in-law, J.J.'s wife, might not want to join the business at all but perhaps feels pressured to do so.

One of the reasons for having in-laws at family meetings is so that they will understand the family's mission and how the family business fits into that mission. It gives them the opportunity to be supportive of their spouses, the business, and their spouses' roles within the business.

■ *The consultant's role.* For those of us who work with family enterprises, keeping an open mind about what will and will not work is important. I am constantly surprised at the great solutions families develop to deal with their challenges. Some families assume that as long as they set guidelines on the business side, they can make the situation work when a qualified in-law applies to enter the business. Families need to know, however, that every decision they make can potentially create complications in other areas. The important point is for families to think through the issues, and those of us working with these families need to help them objectify and think through their decisions—not make the decisions for them.

Conclusion

Family members who share assets (i.e., members of a family enterprise) face challenges not only in managing the enterprise but also in managing family dynamics. This relationship system can be thought of as three separate but interlocking circles representing the ownership, business, and relationship aspects of the system. Thus, when families contemplate making any change (such as transferring ownership of the business from the first to the second generation), the impact the decision has on all three circles must be taken into account.

For those of us working in the family business field, this transfer from the first to the second generation is crucial because it creates a model and sets the tone for all transfers that follow. Our role is to help families objectify the family business succession process and to motivate them to think about the implications of their decisions in this regard. The reality is that a family enterprise will survive in subsequent generations only through a concerted effort by the family to establish regular family and shareholder meetings to discuss the complicated issues surrounding family business wealth.

Question and Answer Session

Fredda Herz Brown

Question: In the case study, what is the children's exit strategy if they leave the business now? Their 7.5 percent ownership interest is not useful to them if they cannot get the cash out.

Brown: One of the central issues in any kind of family enterprise is how to cash out over time. Families need to address that issue early on to avoid the possibility of a major lawsuit centered on the valuation of the business.

Question: How can we help our clients express their insecurities about money so that we can help them with some of their concerns?

Brown: One way to get people to look at the issue of what money means to them is to ask them to think about the way money has been handled in their families over the generations. Once they have thought about this issue, you can ask, for example, whether there were differences in what the girls and boys were taught about money. You can map the issues of money, control, and authority for several generations and begin to understand the source of their insecurities. Only then will you be able to address these insecurities and anticipate them when you talk about the transfer of wealth and/or the business.

Question: If the founder is resistant to facilitating or developing a succession plan, what are alternative strategies?

Brown: Founders seem much less resistant to leaving the enterprise than they used to be. Business has become so difficult that people want to get out. Nevertheless, sometimes the founder is not willing to take the first step toward a transition. I've discovered that working with the next generation on its vision for the business and on negotiations with the founder often makes the founder less resistant to moving ahead with the transition because the founder sees the children becoming more active in the business.

Question: Do you have any statistics on how many family businesses fail in the second or third generation, and why do you think these failures occur?

Brown: Such statistics are readily available by going to the Family Firm Institute's Web site at www.ffi.org. One-third of the family businesses in the United States, according to the current statistics, make it to the second generation, and 12 percent, to the third generation; only 3 percent survive into the fourth generation and beyond.

A number of reasons exists for those not-so-rosy statistics. Most people say this lack of success stems from the unique, complicated issues that family businesses must deal with, but many nonfamily businesses going through a transition do not make it either. In fact, the statistics on first- or second-generation transitions in any kind of closely held business are not good—about a quarter of these businesses fail.

A family business, however, does have some unique reasons for not succeeding. A family business might not make it if estate-planning issues have not been adequately resolved and/or if family relationship issues have not been worked through well enough to allow for a graceful transition. Frequently, the next generation is simply not prepared to take over the business and make it work well. Therefore, developing leadership skills among the family members is a significant issue for increasing the longevity of family businesses.

Future Strategies for Private Wealth Management

John Philip Coghlan
Vice Chairman
The Charles Schwab Corporation
San Francisco

> In the past, only the ultra wealthy sought investment advice, and when they did, they went to Wall Street firms. Today, more households have more money, and they are looking for guidance from a number of providers on how to invest their wealth. With this change in clientele, namely the rise of the mass affluent and the engaged investor, firms stand to benefit from a surge in the demand for advice but must be careful not to overload investors with information; the use of technology will be pivotal in servicing this growing segment of the market.

At this conference, we have been immersed in the multiple aspects of private wealth management, such as tax-efficient investing and wealth-transfer planning, which are incredibly important topics, but I would like to focus my remarks on the client. Many portfolio managers and advisors deal with institutional clients, but at this conference we are going one level deeper to the individual investor.

So, what about these clients? What is on their minds? They are worried. Many have unrealistic expectations about their investments. They are overwhelmed with information. They are very demanding. They are constantly comparing advisors with their competitors, and they do not know whom to trust.

Let me explain. Americans who are now seeking investment advice have emerged from the 1990s more affluent, more investment savvy, and more comfortable with technology than any previous cohort of investors. But they have also been chastened. They rode the wave of the stock market boom for nearly a decade—and saw much of it collapse in just over a year. Certainly, the combination of "dot bomb" and what I now understand to be "the recession just ended" has given Americans second thoughts about investing. And September 11 has probably changed their perceptions permanently. How so? I think American investors remain optimistic, hopeful, and ambitious. It is part of their character. But their tolerance for risk has declined, which is a significant development for those of us in the asset management business. We have seen that decline in risk tolerance take many forms. Americans are less comfortable abroad. They are less secure at home; this risk avoidance can be seen at airports, sports arenas, and malls. The country has drawn inward.

It is impossible to talk about the attitudes of individual investors toward financial security without taking this new attitude of risk avoidance into consideration. I am certain most advisors have seen it already in their clients' behavior, just as we have at Schwab. Yes, there is evidence of the kind Alan Greenspan cited to indicate that the economy may already have begun to recover. But at Schwab, the continued stagnation of retail investor activity (in early 2002) has kept us from reacting optimistically to these reports of improvement.

Two Grand Changes in Wealth Management

Whether the economy recovers quickly or slowly will not change the fact that what we saw in the 1990s were two watershed developments in the investment industry. These developments were sea changes on the landscape of wealth and have very important implications. The first is the rise of "mass affluence." The second is the rise of the "engaged investor."

Mass Affluent. Not that long ago, the image of the typical retail client seeking help in managing his wealth was Richie Rich or Daddy Warbucks. That image disappeared over the past decade or so. Certainly, there are still plenty of very wealthy individuals, but the most significant development has been the rapid growth of households with *investable assets* (excluding personal residence) of $100,000 to $1 million. That may not sound like much money, but these people have good incomes and perhaps a small amount of family money. They save. Their kids are going to college. And they compose a new and important part of the affluent market. This market has been growing for some time, and it has been growing significantly.

The affluent investor was once the exclusive purview of Wall Street firms and some top-drawer private banks and trust companies, but there was nothing "mass" or populist about this type of investor. Technology and the spread of wealth, however, have made it possible to serve affluent investors in many ways, thereby creating a big opportunity in this market and a new competitive playing field.

As **Figure 1** and **Table 1** demonstrate, the number of affluent Americans is still going through a boom, and Baby Boomers have a lot to do with it. Today, Baby Boomers control about 27 percent of assets in the United States. In the next 20 years, that number is projected to increase to 57 percent. For those of us in the investment advisory world, that growth means this cohort will become an even more important part of our business. And more good news is coming from the demographics. Every segment of the affluent market is growing, but as **Table 2** demonstrates, the segment growing fastest is the one with $500,000 to $1 million in investable assets.

Those numbers will redefine our business. In some respects, they will make it easier. After all, those who have often been considered high net worth—those with, say, $5 million or $10 million in assets—were not so easy to serve. They required a tremendous amount of customized attention and many face-to-face meetings. And the competition for these clients has been, and continues to be, ferocious. Make no mistake. These very wealthy individuals are also growing in number and getting wealthier. But the huge new opportunity with the affluent will be through unit volume. Fortunately, the combination of technology and people will allow us to bring sophisticated solutions to the mass affluent at a reasonable cost.

Engaged Investor. The second great shift that has taken place in investing over the past decade is the rise of the engaged investor. This change is another earthquake shaking up the world of investment management. The world of the passive affluent

Figure 1. Growth in Households by Asset Cohort

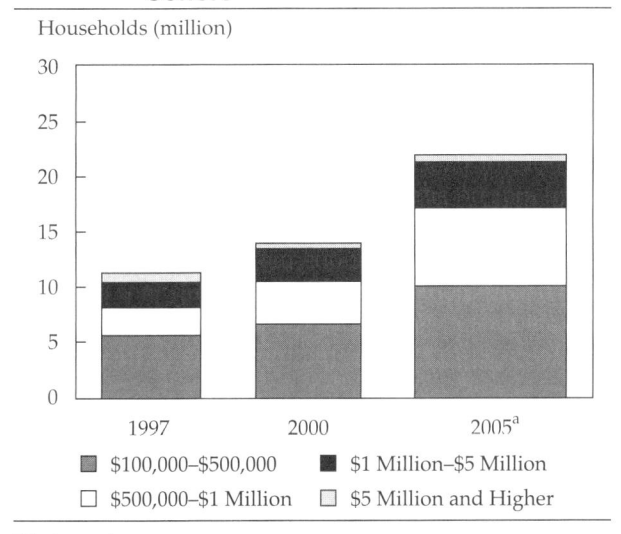

Table 1. Compound Annual Growth Rate by Asset Cohort

Asset Cohort	1997–2000	2000–05[a]
$100,000–$500,000	8%	8%
$500,000–$1 million	13	13
$1 million–$5 million	10	10
$5 million and higher	11	11
Overall	9	10

[a] Estimated.

Source: Based on Business Systems Group's analysis of SpectremGroup data.

Table 2. Number of U.S. Households with Various Levels of Wealth, 1997–2005 (millions)

Amount of Wealth	1997	2000	2005[a]
Emerging affluent ($100,000–$499,000)	5.3	6.8	10.0
Mass affluent ($500,000–$1 million)	2.5	3.8	7.4
Upper affluent ($1 million and higher)	2.4	3.3	5.4
Total	10.2	13.9	22.8

[a] Estimated.

Source: Based on data from SpectremGroup and VIP Forum.

[a] Estimated.
Source: Business Systems Group's analysis of SpectremGroup data.

investor who hands over his or her money and gets a quarterly update will become less and less common.

Engaged investors are redefining advisors' relationships with their clients. When Chuck Schwab first opened his discount brokerage firm in 1975, the investment world was neatly divided between two types of investors, the "delegators" and the "self-directed investors." The delegators perhaps had an account at Merrill Lynch & Company or U.S. Trust or another financial advisor they spoke to periodically.[1] The self-directed investors were clients like Schwab's—people who considered themselves sufficiently experienced in the marketplace to invest on their own.

But in the past 10 years, as the Baby Boomers have begun to enter their prime investing years, advisors have seen an extremely important change. Today, the largest and fastest growing segment of the market is composed of "validators." These are the people who want to retain the feeling of control over their investments. They have a sense about what they want to do, but they want to *validate* their perspectives with the advice of a professional. This is a subtle distinction, but an important one. Validators do not mind if someone else ultimately makes the decision or even "pulls the trigger." But they do not want to give up that sense of control and involvement. These validators *are* the engaged investors. They are increasingly becoming the dominant part of the affluent market.

As **Figure 2** shows, the validators are the largest category of investors in most of the asset brackets—

[1] U.S. Trust is a wholly owned subsidiary of The Charles Schwab Corporation.

from less than $300,000 to just less than $5 million. Although they are seeking investment advice, they are very different from their parents' generation. For one thing, they are technologically savvy. They may trade or access their accounts online. They surf the Web for research. They spread their money across more than one institution. They are also younger, and their expectations are higher than those of the affluent investors of the past.

But whatever the asset level, at least two other things can be said about these validators. They want choices when it comes to investing. And they want to be involved in the decision making, which is why these validators—these engaged investors—pose substantial challenges as advisors try to serve them well.

Implications

The rise of the mass affluent and the engaged investor are two big shifts that have occurred in the asset management industry. What are the implications of these changes? What further changes will they trigger? Let me suggest just three:
- advice surge,
- information overload, and
- technology imperative.

Advice Surge. The bull may have been driven from the market, but a bull market certainly exists for financial advice. And it is not hard to figure out why this is true. The bursting of the technology bubble,

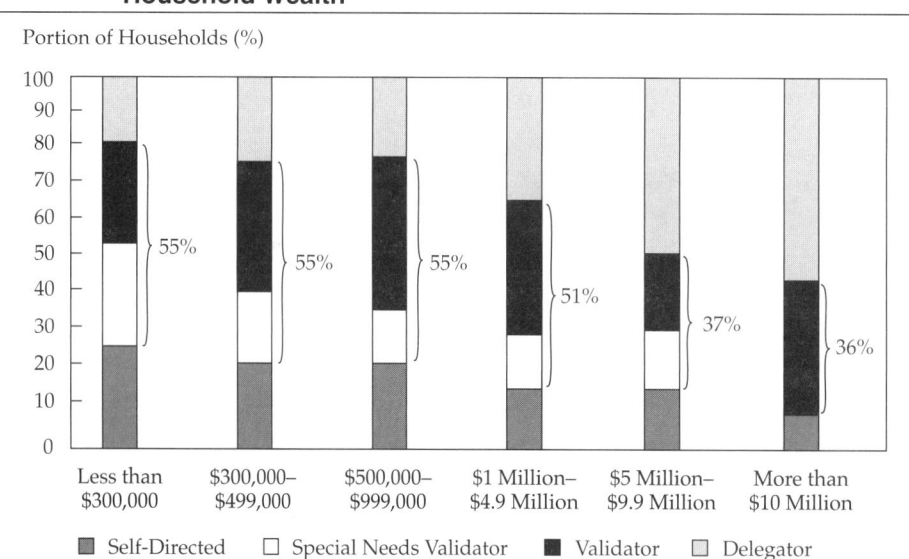

Figure 2. Percentage of Households in Each Investor Behavior Category by Household Wealth

Source: Based on data from SpectremGroup.

the volatility of the market, and the general uncertainty of the economy have changed attitudes among clients and potential clients.

Advice had a bad rap during the dot-com run up. To the first wave of online traders, "advice" was something their fathers needed. After all, even the empowered online cab driver had his island in the Caribbean. But it is remarkable what a 3,000-point drop in the Nasdaq can do. Suddenly, every type of investor is seeking advice. If the advice is sensible, that change is probably a good thing for everyone.

This trend actually began even before the bubble burst in March of 2000. According to data from SpectremGroup, the VIP Forum, and Schwab Market Research, from 1998 to 2000, the proportion of affluent households considering themselves "self directed" dropped from 26 percent to 18 percent—not good news for the old Charles Schwab. Meanwhile, the use of professional advisors grew from 56 percent to 67 percent of the affluent market. In fact, as **Table 3** indicates, the independent advisors and investment managers—not the banks or the traditional brokers—are gaining the most from this trend. They are seeing their businesses increase more than any other segment of the investment world as more and more people are looking for advice.

Table 3. Growth in Providers of Advice

Provider	1998	2000
Attorney, insurance agent, other	2%	4%
Banker	3	3
Accountant	5	3
Mutual fund	3	4
Discount/online	1	5
Investment manager	7	13
Financial planner	9	11
Traditional broker	26	24

Source: Based on data from the VIP Forum, the Federal Reserve, Cerulli Associates, and Schwab Analysis.

According to Cerulli Associates, assets controlled by independent advisors will continue to grow at 25 percent a year for the next three years, and I think this finding is great news for the consumer. Not so long ago, private advice was available only to relatively few people. What is happening with the rise of the mass affluent is a "democratization" of financial advice. The tremendous demand from the mass affluent is allowing new players to flourish. Smaller firms and independent advisors that can meet the demands of the mass affluent are creating an accessible and affordable service for the millions who have seen their portfolios expand. At one time, they would have had no choice but to seek assistance at a Wall Street brokerage firm. Today, even those firms have withdrawn from a portion of this market, unable to profitably serve relationships less than $1 million. That is a huge change. In a way, traditional providers are abandoning the playing field for the mass affluent.

The democratization of financial advice creates a great opportunity for many advisors, but it does not come without a challenge. This mass affluent, engaged client is a demanding one. For one, her expectations remain high. She has lived through the 1990s and enjoyed seven fat years in the stock market. She probably is not prepared for the less robust returns investors might see over the next few years. In fact, a recent Gallup/Paine Webber survey found that investors still expect a 14 percent long-term return on their investments.

Managers might think a 14 percent expectation in a single-digit market environment could engender the kind of difficult conversations with clients that they remember from the years when the market was up 20 percent and they were only up 14 percent. But I think the situation will be different. Based on the conversations we have had with investors at Schwab, we think clients' return expectations are being adjusted downward. The combination of the Nasdaq crash and September 11 has put everyone on notice that the volatility of any aspect of their lives is much greater than they had previously believed.

The guidance that investors now seek has also changed. A long-term orientation and the preaching advisors did about diversification was lost in the mania. A more suitable holistic view that provides a context and a framework for investing is definitely back; it is actually what investors are asking for. Certainly, that holistic view is what investors have always sought from U.S. Trust and firms like it. It is the cornerstone of their approach. But the trend is also visible in the much more transaction-oriented Schwab client base. At Schwab, we are amazed that even our own retail client base has been seeking advice at such a growing rate. In the year 2001 alone, Schwab referred more than 14,000 clients to independent investment advisors through our AdvisorSource program. During the year, more than 4,000 people who had been previously referred established relationships with these independent advisors—a total of $5.3 billion in new assets managed by those advisors. The total managed by advisors simply from assets referred to them by Schwab now stands at $13 billion.

Clearly, the network of independent investment advisors with whom we have built a relationship is an irreplaceable asset for our firm. In every way, we are trying to share our technology, our back office, and our clients with these advisors. For investors who cannot meet those advisors' minimums or who choose not to pay an ongoing fee, Schwab has established another program, offering a one-time portfolio consultation for only $500. Over the course of the year, more than 45,000 investors paid that fee to understand whether their portfolios were constructed to meet their investment objectives.

I offer these stories not to tout our offering or its success but in astonishment that such latent demand exists in the mass affluent market and that it has showed up at Schwab, the historical home of the self-directed investor. Certainly, we could note the "independent and objective" nature of the advice being sought. But that is only part of the picture. The additional challenge is being able to provide this advice in a way that is objective and independent, certainly, but also very personalized while still being affordable for the client and cost-effective for the provider—no small task!

Information Overload. The relationship between financial advisors and their clients brings me to the next implication I want to discuss: information overload. The world that was once neatly divided into brokerage houses, banks, and investment houses has disappeared. The demise of Glass–Steagall and the growing sophistication of clients have contributed to the elimination of these neat divisions. Clients are not only wealthier and more engaged in their investing; they are less likely to turn to just one source for their insights. And the result is a Niagara Falls of financial information—lots of information, very little knowledge or wisdom.

Information overload—it can be seen whenever consumers try to compare health care plans, insurance packages, or mutual funds. Even the engaged investor that I have been describing can absorb only so much information. Time is also a valuable commodity to them, which is where wealth managers can make a difference. Increasingly, the affluent client is looking for a "trusted navigator." This model is very different from the old Wall Street broker. The client wants someone who is independent and objective, whose motivation is the client's best interests, and who has the professional background to make sense of all the different streams of information.

Most firms call this position the "quarterback," and whether they are Wall Street firms, trust companies, private banks, or independent advisors, they are all trying to move to that same space. A number of firms are having success, some by populating the asset and liability sides of the client balance sheet with proprietary products.

As advisors know, the more legs to the stool of the relationship, the more stable the relationship will be. The problem is that in some ways, advisors are giving clients the solutions the advisors want rather than the solutions the clients are seeking. Clients know that no single provider is likely to be the best solution for every aspect of their financial puzzle. It flies in the face of reason. In addition, many clients are concerned about having their financial relationship be solely with a single institution—simply from the perspective of the concentration of risk. Finally, clients often see conflicts within the model—lots of conflicts. Suppose a fee-based relationship is established to eliminate commission conflicts. There still can be fine-print issues around double dipping, possible research conflicts around equity recommendations, potential conflicts about fixed-income inventories, and arbitrary and annoying limits to portability stemming from the proprietary nature of products.

Table 4 illustrates, I believe, the many reasons why a client would want to keep his or her money with several institutions. This study shows that the typical wealthy investor has money in many different instruments, and in many different "pots." And such an investor typically uses multiple financial service providers to serve these needs.

Table 4. Distribution of Investable Assets

Type of Account	Total Affluent Market (thousands)[a]	Wealth Market (thousands)[b]
Deposits	$ 97	$148
Stocks and bonds	197	426
Mutual funds	149	271
Alternative investments	9	13
Investment management accounts	180	354
Managed trust and custody	203	493
Rollover IRAs	118	222
Other IRAs	107	216
Other investable assets	73	150

[a]$500,000 and higher in net worth, not including private residence.

[b]$1 million and higher in net worth, not including private residence.

Source: SpectremGroup's 2001 affluent investor research study.

Advisors should not complain about this situation. In fact, it probably should be encouraged. What advisors are seeing is the death of the all-knowing, constantly reliable single advisor. Clients want to shop around. They want to hedge their bets. They want to diversify in many ways—including in the institutions on which they rely—which is where *aggregation* or *consolidation* comes in. These have been buzzwords in the industry for the past few years. In their earliest iterations, they meant giving the client and the advisor the ability to look across accounts of all types—regardless of where that money was invested—to get a comprehensive view, which is important but not all that exciting. In its earliest versions, clients were able to view the data but could not do anything with them.

That situation has changed. The industry is certainly very close to the day when it will be able to offer clients the ability to slice and dice their holdings any way they want—without the sneaker brigade in the background that makes it possible today. For example, they will be able to analyze how their equity picks at Merrill are doing against their equity picks at U.S. Trust to directly compare taxable accounts (or tax-deferred accounts), to create personalized benchmarks, and to understand which providers are exceeding those benchmarks and which are not. And they will be able to perform holistic, real-time wealth planning, liberated from much of the tremendous manual activity that today supports that effort.

So, what is transpiring is the harnessing of technology to help clients slice through the overload of information and get to wisdom that is entirely client specific. It will quickly become commoditized, will necessarily be transportable, and, as such, will raise the bar of expectation for everyone involved, which does not sound that great for providers, especially when some of the ramifications are considered. When clients have an easy time gauging performance, they are likely to be willing to move to those who are exceeding their benchmarks. This situation may be good for clients, but it can be quite hard on their service providers.

Those who may be more insulated from harm are those who develop the role of the trusted navigator. They can more easily welcome the tools allowing this comparison. When they take the additional step of contributing to a deeper and richer understanding of the possibilities and the limits, they may well be considered indispensable. That transformation may seem easier for independent investment advisors. For many traditional competitors in the marketplace, the sales structures and product strategies they use make this trusted navigator role more difficult to attain.

Technology Imperative. The third implication I want to touch on is what I call the "technology imperative." At Schwab, we have had a front-row seat at the financial technology revolution for the past 10 years. We started experimenting with online trading even before the Web took hold of the country. Today, our Web site remains one of the largest and most secure commercial Web sites in the world. We have 4.3 million active online accounts with some $340 billion in assets. Nearly 82 percent of our clients use our Web site to do research or to trade. For our firm, the first phase of the tech revolution is over. We are no longer focused on getting people to switch to Schwab.com but, rather, on how we can augment our client relationships by building technology into each and every one of them.

For many of the players on the scene, there is much room for improvement. Although most of the thousands of independent investment advisors with whom I work have Web sites, many sites are static brochure-ware. Even the far more substantial financial institutions offer clients very limited capability, which is increasingly becoming a problem for those who would try to serve the mass affluent.

Let me illustrate my point with a few statistics from a recent Schwab Institutional survey conducted in conjunction with the SpectremGroup.

- 78 percent of affluent households say they use the Internet from home. (That is a good sign.)
- 61 percent of these households report they have used the Internet for account management once during the past year.
- 24 percent of the affluent market traded securities online at least once last year.
- 18 percent said they paid bills online.

I draw two general conclusions from these numbers. First, affluent households have just started getting their feet wet in the online world of financial services, so there is still plenty of room to grow. Second, if firms want to keep these clients, they have to be providing a fairly sophisticated technology offering. The relationship may not depend on it today, but it will become increasingly important.

Many investment professionals will not like the following assertion. Most investment advisors and portfolio managers do two things well and enjoy doing those two things: cultivating trusted relationships with clients and managing money. The problem is that developing technology services for the engaged client can be time consuming and expensive. The last thing most investment professionals or relationship managers want is to have to design a Web site or evaluate their Web site's scalability or security features.

Serving the mass affluent is a conundrum. The unit volume may be strong, but the delivery of wealth management services in the past has been people intensive and, therefore, costly. The situation only gets more dire if firms now target mass affluent clients who are less able to pay for all the expensive people needed to serve them. Technology purports to be the solution. It allows the leveraging of human talent and puts more of the tools that transform information into knowledge in the hands of the client. The trusted navigator, in a sense, is increasingly placed in a position to transform that knowledge into wisdom. But the difficulty in putting this all together is the cost of technology. And even though we all hope that the cost will decline in the future, I never met anyone who had that experience! Although one piece of technology leadership may become commoditized, the next advance in client-centric technology is always on the horizon.

The point is that, even though the mass affluent market represents a marvelous opportunity for many firms, it will take a powerful combination of advice delivery, information management, and technology to be successful in that market.

Summary

The new world is about the huge opportunity that lies before advisors with the engaged investor in a new mass affluent market. This new type of client wants a different kind of service from what advisors are used to providing, which is a good thing because the economics of the old model simply does not work in this market.

Advisors will have to provide a more open architecture environment, offer greater portability, be tolerant of their clients' having multiple investment service relationships, and use a seamless combination of technology and people to provide a high-value client experience in a cost-effective manner. Certainly, meeting the needs of these clients will be one of the most intellectually and professionally challenging tasks advisors will ever face. But make no mistake; the opportunity is enormous. And as we have discovered over and over again at Schwab, keeping our eye on the interests of the client—not on the market, technology, or investment trends, but on the client—is the most reliable formula for success.

Question and Answer Session

John Philip Coghlan

Question: Who will provide the nirvana of consolidation of account information (the Merrills, the MyCFO.coms, or the Schwabs)?

Coghlan: Everybody is working (and racing) toward consolidation. MyCFO was the early leader, and it was racing with a group of technology companies toward the right place. But I don't think being first matters as much as being pointed in the right direction and actually getting there. Certainly, a Merrill or Schwab has the resources to make consolidation happen. Increasingly, the walls are coming down between institutions, and much depends on the willingness of clients and firms to share account data.

If one of my clients says, "I want you to share my data—after all it is not your data, it is my data—with XYZ firm," I will. The friction evident today in terms of a firm's willingness to provide that service will disappear because the entire market is moving toward the same place. Again, a particular firm may get there first, but the ultimate product has to be portable over time and can't be proprietary.

Question: Serving clients who require more involvement in the management of their investments implies higher costs and lower profits for their advisors. How does Schwab deal with this challenge, and how will it change the business realities for smaller advisors?

Coghlan: I disagree with that premise. The business we have had with investment advisors has gone from about an 80 bp business to a 25 bp business in the past seven or eight years, and yet that business remains profitable. We have invested with those advisors in the necessary technology, which has driven down the costs.

The secret in dealing with individuals lies in finding ways to lever your involvement with them. We studied how advisors spend their time. Too much time, for example, is spent on client services that are not about acquiring or strengthening relationships but about answering low-value-added questions. That practice has to be stopped, and clients need resources for finding easy ways to get that same information. Doing so saves a ton of money and, from the clients' perspective, creates more proactive and convenient services that are available whenever clients need them.

Question: Is it information overload or lack of financial savvy and education that drives the demand for advice?

Coghlan: It is clearly a product of both information overload and lack of financial know-how, but it also stems from a void of credibility or trust. Information is available, but for clients, it is an issue of "What information do I believe?" Investment advisors, by virtue of their market relationships and knowledge, thus get a chance to build client relationships based on being the person the client trusts.

Question: How does U.S. Trust fit into the new world of investing you have described?

Coghlan: Schwab acquired U.S. Trust in 2000, and U.S. Trust fits into the new investment scene in two ways. First is the name itself. I cannot think of two letters (U and S) and one word (trust) that would make a better brand. The company is underappreciated and not well known. Most people have heard of it and know that it is old and good, but that is all. We have the expertise to help U.S. Trust build that brand into what we hope will be the preeminent wealth management brand in the United States.

The second way U.S. Trust fits into the new order has to do with its people and institutional market wisdom. In addition to brand building, we're adding technology capability so that U.S. Trust can appeal not only to old money (U.S. Trust's average client holds $7 million in investable assets) but also to the engaged investor, the technologically savvy younger investor, not the mass affluent, which has not been U.S. Trust's business focus. In addition, we want to absorb U.S. Trust's market wisdom, which could be a brand within Schwab that we use to attract a broader audience.

©2002, AIMR®

Selected Publications

AIMR

Benchmarks and Attribution Analysis, 2001

Best Execution and Portfolio Performance, 2001

Core-Plus Bond Management, 2001

Developments in Quantitative Investment Models, 2001

Equity Research and Valuation Techniques, 2002

Ethical Issues for Today's Firm, 2000

Evolution in Equity Markets: Focus on Asia, 2001

Fixed-Income Management for the 21st Century, 2002

Global Bond Management II: The Search for Alpha, 2000

Hedge Fund Management, 2002

Investment Counseling for Private Clients II, 2000

Investment Counseling for Private Clients III, 2001

Investment Firms: Trends and Issues, 2001

Organizational Challenges for Investment Firms, 2002

Practical Issues in Equity Analysis, 2000

The Technology Industry: Impact of the Internet, 2000

Research Foundation

Common Determinants of Liquidity and Trading, 2001
by Tarun Chordia, Richard Roll, and Avanidhar Subrahmanyam

Country, Sector, and Company Factors in Global Equity Portfolios, 2001
by Peter J.B. Hopkins and C. Hayes Miller, CFA

Earnings: Measurement, Disclosure, and the Impact on Equity Valuation, 2000
by D. Eric Hirst and Patrick E. Hopkins

International Financial Contagion: Theory and Evidence in Evolution, 2002
by Roberto Rigobon

Real Options and Investment Valuation, 2002
by Don M. Chance, CFA, and Pamela P. Peterson, CFA

Risk Management, Derivatives, and Financial Analysis under SFAS No. 133, 2001
by Gary L. Gastineau, Donald J. Smith, and Rebecca Todd, CFA

The Role of Monetary Policy in Investment Management, 2000
by Gerald R. Jensen, Robert R. Johnson, CFA, and Jeffrey M. Mercer

Term-Structure Models Using Binomial Trees, 2001
by Gerald W. Buetow, Jr., CFA, and James Sochacki

The Welfare Effects of Soft Dollar Brokerage: Law and Economics, 2000
by Stephen M. Horan, CFA, and D. Bruce Johnsen